Elaine Johnson

D1085681

The
IMPOSSIBLE

The IMPOSSIBLE

Overcoming Unthinkable Abuse

Ruth Redcay

It is with great joy and pleasure that I dedicate this book to my two beautiful daughters Jennifer and Angie.

Jennifer and her husband, Markus, always believed in me and encouraged me to share my story to help others.

Angie and her husband, Mark, are my cheerleaders as well and told me often what a great mom I was and am.

I love you Jennifer, Markus, Angie, and Mark!

Some names and identifying details have been
changed to protect the privacy of individuals.

The Impossible: Overcoming Unthinkable Abuse

© 2019 by Ruth Redcay

All rights reserved. No part of this book may be reproduced or transmitted in any form or by any means, electronic or mechanical, including photocopying, recording or by any information storage and retrieval system, without permission in writing from the copyright owner.

Published by Clovercroft Publishing, Franklin, Tennessee

Taken from *My Utmost for His Highest*® by Oswald Chambers, edited by James Reimann, © 1992 by Oswald Chambers Publications Assn., Ltd., and used by permission of Discovery House, Grand Rapids MI 49501. All rights reserved.

Cover and Interior Design by Adept Content Solutions

Printed in the United States of America

ISBN (Print)   978-0-578-47983-5
ISBN (eBook)   978-0-578-47984-2

Contents

Foreword
by Dr. Brenda Wright

Ruth Redcay's life has been a walking, breathing testimony to the absolute faithfulness of God's promise when He said, "I will never leave you nor forsake you" (Hebrews 13:5b). I've had the privilege of walking alongside Ruth during some of her darkest days. She experienced great depths of abandonment and despair, during which she battled with: excruciating emotional pain resulting from betrayal; many fears that were at times paralyzing; depths of anger that even surprised her; and multiple questions to God asking "why!!"

I would describe Ruth as a woman of great perseverance and courage (Joshua 1:9); when nothing made any sense and she had no clue how she was going to make it, she refused to let go of God, desperately depending on His strength and His step-by-step guidance, allowing Him to be a lamp to her feet and a light to her path (Psalm 119:105).

This book is not filled with religious piety and platitudes—they don't work! Ruth is a real, authentic, flesh-and-blood woman who has experienced the lowest of the lows, but she is also a living testimony to God's promise that "nothing is too difficult for Him," and she showed that she "could do all things through Christ who strengthened her" (Philippians 4:13).

So whoever is reading this book, please know that God is no respecter of persons. . . . He has no favorites. What He has done (and is still doing) in and through Ruth, He can also do for you in your particular situation. In her fear, Ruth chose to willingly surrender, to trust her life and her future to God. This book will show you what that process looked like for her.

Blessings,
Brenda Wright

Acknowledgments

I want to thank my friend Dave Landis, who spent many hours editing the first draft of this book. I greatly appreciated his feedback as I wrote.

I am grateful for my pastor Lanny Kilgore for his encouragement and giving me an opportunity to share my story at church.

I want to thank all of my friends, family, and others who through the years kept telling me that I needed to write a book. They played a big part in this book becoming a reality.

Last but not least, I want to thank my best friend, Anne Allgyer. She has walked by my side through thick and thin for over 30 years. She believed in me, encouraged me, and never gave up on me even when I wanted to give up on myself. She is a beautiful person to whom I owe a debt of gratitude.

Note to the Reader

To understand some of the nuances of this story, it is important to get a bit of a handle on life in rural Lancaster County, Pennsylvania, among the "plain folk," where I was raised.

Some think of the Pennsylvania Dutch as being largely German. Other sources say many of the Mennonites actually emigrated from Switzerland but are of German descent. The story goes that the Mennonites ran to Switzerland to be able to have religious freedom, but they still speak a dialect of German called Pennsylvania Dutch.

The Mennonites and Amish are, and were, mostly patriarchal societies. That was gleaned from the Bible, where it states that a woman should honor and obey her husband. Unfortunately, most did not read the rest of that chapter and verse, where it states the "man shall love his wife as Christ loved the church."

Therefore, the man was seldom challenged. As this tale unfolds, you, the modern reader, will be dumbfounded by how such atrocities could befall the young children and wife. How could the wife tolerate such behavior from her husband and her own treatment?

Male dominance was rarely questioned or challenged in the church and the community. In many families, the father was also regarded as a paragon of virtue and self-discipline and he taught his family to be as well.

Understanding the culture of these very pragmatic, fundamentally driven, Bible-oriented folks may help you begin to comprehend how some of the things that happened in this one family could have coexisted with the spiritually driven orientation of the Mennonite sect.

Prologue

I was startled from my sleep, not wanting to look at the clock. Two in the morning! Oh my, this was much too early. Not time to get up yet. Then, once I remembered why I was awake, fear rolled over me like a 12-foot ocean wave coming right at me. There was no way to escape, no place to run. I could feel the grit of sand in my mouth, crushed and held against the ocean floor. Little did I know back then at the tender age of 13 what lay ahead of me. This was just the tip of the iceberg. I would wake up at 2 a.m. for many, many more years to come face to face with unimaginable terror and turmoil beyond what seems imaginable.

Part One

1

This Is Just the Beginning

I was born on March 29, 1951, part of the baby boomer generation. I was the second child and first daughter born to my young parents. They had been married about four years at the time. Over the next eight years, my mother would give birth to eight more children. This would amount to 10 children in a 12-year period. I had five sisters and four brothers. The large number of children so close together would be overwhelming in the best of families. However, as it came to pass, our family would not be anything close to the best.

I sometimes feel as though I have a memory of not wanting to be born. Of course I assume that this feeling is not an actual memory. As I would listen to my mother describe my birth, it did feel like I could identify with what she was saying. She explained that it was a long and difficult labor for her. I was born blue without any breath, giving my mother the impression that I would not make it. To her horror, the nurses whisked me away. After a grueling hour of waiting, my mother was told that I was given oxygen and would make it after all. Not only would I make it, but I would be as healthy as any other.

My first memory of my childhood was around four years of age. That vivid memory came back to me in the form of a violent flashback at around the age of 38. Before that, I barely had any memories of my childhood that I could credit to be real. I did not concern myself with it or think it unusual at the time. As I neared the age of 38, my marriage of 13 years was unraveling before my eyes. I was depressed and very unhappy with my life. I knew that it had to be my husband's fault, of course. What else could it be? I had two beautiful daughters, the unrestricted use of our credit card, a brand-new house, lovely clothes, a good church, and a good circle of friends. It just had to be him, right? He was the enemy. Why wasn't he making me happy? That was the whole reason I got married—to be happy and fulfilled.

As I sat in my therapist's office one day, I had a list of complaints a mile long. I was overly angry and bitter. At the time, it was all directed toward my husband. If he would only get his act together and stop his workaholic lifestyle, things would be fine. He would bring up my childhood and use that against me in any way he could. He just would not let the past be the past no matter how much I would gripe or whine. My wonderful therapist Terri listened intently as I unloaded on her for the entire 50 minutes of my appointment.

"Your time is up for today," she gently interrupted me. "When would you like to schedule your next appointment?"

I was livid! How could she be so calm? She did not even solve one of my problems today and she wants another appointment at $90 an hour? Forget it. I stormed out talking to myself all the way home. Two days later, feeling depressed again and now guilty for my behavior, I called her and made another appointment. That one decision turned out to be much more important and life-changing than I could ever have imagined at the time. I had no clue as to what lay ahead. I am glad I did not know, or I would not have gone back. Terri was my angel. I believe that without her I would have died! God knew what I needed to survive. For the next five years, I would face my past and experience memories that produced great loss, pain, and anger that at times I felt would kill me.

Flashback to before the marital trouble started: My wedding day was two days away from my 25th birthday. It was March 27, 1976. I was very happy and excited for the most part. Underneath it all though lurked a dark secret that Dan, my husband-to-be, knew nothing about. My past and lack of childhood memories would become a huge factor in my marriage problems down the road, which all led to some very poor personal choices and behavior on my part.

As I approached my wedding day, I still had feelings for Allen, an old flame. I had met him a few years earlier and fell really hard for him. Allen was tall, dark, and handsome, and I felt he would be the love of my life. He played guitar and sang, which was also intriguing to me. I thought it was a perfect match made in heaven. I took guitar lessons soon after meeting him to impress him and increase my chances of being with him. We flirted, teased each other, and laughed together often.

But we never did formally date. He started dating a girl I knew from the church that we all attended. I was also dating Dan at the time. I was heartbroken but kept thinking it will not work out with Allen and her or with Dan and me, and I will get Allen back. Allen continued to flirt with me and me with him while we were dating our respective partners, which fed my hope of being with him. A part of me died that day in November 1975 when he married her. I went home and sobbed like never before. Then I got myself together and focused on my current relationship with Dan.

Dan and I got engaged two months down the road. I really did love Dan. He had a great sense of humor, and his laugh was contagious. He was an aspiring entrepreneur and had started his own business, which I found to be quite admirable. He was a good, honest man. We went on a two-week honeymoon to Shenandoah National Park in Virginia and had a wonderful time. I found out soon after we got home, however, that I was pregnant with our first child. I got sick as a dog. I threw up every day like clockwork. There were quite a few days where I had lost count of the times I'd gotten sick. I could not eat and did not want to because it would just come back up. I lost 10 pounds in the first four months due to my lack of interest in eating at the time. In spite of all this, I gave birth to a healthy 8-pound, 1-ounce baby girl.

She was born on January 5, 1977, which was also my father's birthday. He was thrilled to have the first grandchild share his birthday. I myself found it to be interesting. We named her Jennifer Joy, for I felt this was a very joyful moment. Little did anyone know at the time, however, my personal joy would certainly not last. There was an ominous storm brewing from my past that would come crashing down on me and rip my world asunder.

Fast forward to the beginning of May 1977. As far as the weather was concerned, it was beautiful outside. I woke up that day, however, with feelings of fear and a sense of dread. I soon realized the weather was not going to help me shake it. I felt lost and lonely. I turned to God and began to pray.

"Jesus, please help me! I don't know what to do! I have a baby to take care of." I struggled to get myself together with little success. In fact, it got a whole lot worse and I began sobbing and crying. Suddenly the most unexpected thing happened. I heard a voice clear as day say:

"Someone in your family is going to die, but do not be afraid. I am with you always. I will never leave you."

I was taken by surprise but immediately recognized it as the voice of God. I felt momentarily comforted. Then I had a full-blown panic attack thinking that it was God telling me he was taking my baby. I was beside myself and would not leave her out of my sight. I was also worried about my husband. Could it be him? I barely slept, compulsively watching over my family. I moved Jennifer's changing table away from in front of the window, imagining that a bullet could come through the window and hit her. It was three days of pure agonizing terror.

The morning of the fourth day, the phone call came. My brother, just a year younger than me, was dead. Not only that, but he had died of a self-inflicted gunshot wound to the head.

I was stunned but then felt immediate relief that it was not my husband or child. The relief was short-lived as I struggled to accept that my young, handsome brother of only 24 years of age was gone. I was grief-stricken also when I learned that the undertaker felt his body was too destroyed for even the family to view. I could not see him one more time to say goodbye. It was surreal. Only my dad was allowed to see him for identification purposes. He had been named Henry Jr. after my father. When he was born, he had two toes together to form one. This is how my father then identified the body. We knew as a family that he was depressed but had not known to this extent. People in my rural Mennonite community were not privy to all the more modern "signs of depression and possible suicide." Suicide was just not something one did, so we were all oblivious to the warning signs.

My youngest brother, Darrell, took it the hardest. He felt guilty that somehow it was his fault or that he could have done more to prevent it from happening in the first place. I did not know the details till years later when my brother Darrell revealed that Henry had threatened to kill himself beforehand. Henry Jr. owned a hunting rifle. Darrell hid it under his bed to try and keep Henry safe. Henry found it, however, and that was the gun he used. Darrell still struggles at times even now to forgive himself and let it go. Several months later, I wrote a poem about my brother that hangs on the wall of my living room. This is that poem.

In Loving Memory of My Brother, Henry David Redcay
(April 17, 1977)

I loved life and the pastures green, but there were so many problems it seemed.

There was always something that got me down, even with a lot of nice people around.

I didn't want to hurt you or make you blue, I just didn't know what to do.

Well, enough talk of sadness and gloom, there's something better now, and I'll tell you soon.

Only a little can I reveal of the joy and happiness that I now feel.

Don't be sad and sorrow anymore; it is so beautiful on this heavenly shore.

Wonderful Jesus is always by my side, no more need to run and hide.

What more can I say than that's been said, so rest with peace upon your bed.

I don't want you to worry and stew, because I know you will be coming here too.

Sample. Authorship for this poem has been claimed in several different names.

It is still a tragedy when I think about it today, but God has given me the assurance that Henry is in heaven with Jesus Whom he loved. He left a note for all of his things to be given *"to Back to the Bible broadcast."* This was a program on a Christian radio station that he liked. It was a very difficult time in my life, but the words that God spoke to me earlier now truly comforted me. I knew I was loved and not alone in my grief. Looking back, I see the reason for those words from God.

I had no idea back then that there would be two more untimely deaths in my family. The last one, in 1999, left me so much under a mountain of loss and grief that it threatened my own life.

2

A Damaged Youth

I was the first daughter in my family. There would be two more boys before another girl. I was Daddy's little princess. I do not remember as much about my mother as I do about my father. He always wanted me to be with him. We would go for walks to get our mail. When it got dark on the farm, we went outside on the huge lawn to catch lightning bugs and put them in jars.

The farm where I lived as a child was near West Chester, Pennsylvania. It was a very country setting. We lived on a long lane lined with big oak trees. It was a 123-acre farm. The closest farms around us belonged to rich people who bred race horses. There were many beautiful horse farms nearby. No development or noise—mostly hay and cornfields. We had a big farm house surrounded by huge oak trees. There was lots of shade and cool breezes in the summer. We had no need for air conditioning. This is where I lived all my life until going to New York in 1967.

Money was tight in those days, but once in a great while we made homemade ice cream. We took turns cranking the wooden ice cream maker by hand until it was too hard to turn. Then my strong father did the final strokes until the ice cream was done just perfectly. What a treat this was for a little farm girl! Almost every Sunday after church we had a packed picnic lunch. My dad drove around until we found a school, church, or park. We spread out a large multicolored Cherokee Indian blanket to sit on while we ate. I thought this blanket was the softest, most beautiful thing I had ever seen. Then we would play softball or just run around having fun. Those were the most innocent and happy memories of my childhood. I had no idea that my childhood was about to end, that my innocence would be robbed from me forever, and that I would be forced to grow up much too fast.

Years later, I would have many questions and no answers as to why my world turned upside down.

Where was my mother?

Why were there no photos of her holding me?

Where was everyone?

I still have nagging questions that will never have answers. Questions I've learned to make peace with, but still haunt me in quiet times with wonderment and sadness.

I was about eight years old when I became aware that something felt wrong with Dad and me. He was demanding that we spend more and more alone time together away from the rest of my brothers and sisters. His back rubs were way too long and annoying. Then he would begin to rub my bottom. My stomach was in knots. I knew even as a small child this touch was not right. He would reach under my clothes and give me a front massage including my breasts. I started to cry and tell him to stop. He paid no attention.

"This is our secret," he said. "Do not tell anyone. I love you more than the rest. You are special and very pretty."

He said he wanted me to feel good. I was feeling anything but good. I did not know what to do. I began to feel lonely and afraid. I had also developed physical complications. I had severe constipation problems, stomach pains, and bed-wetting that continued well into my teen years. I remember being so embarrassed by this and trying desperately to hide it. So from the age of eight to 12, during those four years, the progression of abuse continued and escalated. As my body developed, my father became more and more bold. The stage was set. I learned years later that this abuse process is called "grooming the victim." My life was about to take a very dark and ominous turn.

Life on the farm was hard. We got up at 4 a.m. to milk the cows. By 7:30 a.m. the school bus came. The walk out the lane took 15 minutes. All that we had time for was a change of clothes and a mad dash for the bus. We had no shower, only a bathtub, which got used once a week. Saturday night was always bath night for everyone.

I had five sisters and Mom put us all in the bathtub together. About six inches of water was run. Then it went like an assembly line. My mom shampooed each head of hair. Then, with a pitcher, she poured water over us to rinse. Then, with one washcloth, she washed and rinsed the rest of us. All of this was very fast, especially in the wintertime, as we had no heat upstairs. Then the four boys got in. Many times they did not even get fresh water but used what we girls were in. As we all got older, the protest got louder about this arrangement. I am sure it changed over time, but I have no memory of it. When bath time was finished, we laid out our Sunday clothes for church the next morning.

Our whole family went to a little Mennonite church in Parkesburg, Pennsylvania. We went every Sunday no matter what. The family car was stuffed. Back then, there were no seatbelts and we sat on each other's laps. The older kids held the younger ones. I dreaded Sunday morning because of all the yelling and screaming that went into getting 10 children ready for church. I was also embarrassed because most times we were late. I cannot imagine now how all this was done. Of course, Sunday was no day off for milking the cows. What an insane childhood it was, and the insanity was far from over.

In school, I was made fun of. They called me "Germs" and said I smelled bad. Looking back, I am sure it was true, but at the time I was really hurt and shy. I did not have many friends and kept my distance from people. I had one girlfriend who gave me gum one day and I thought I died and went to heaven. I felt so loved by one stick of gum. I am amazed today as I look back that I actually got good grades in school. I have no idea how considering all that was going on at home. I don't remember any of my teachers. I know now it had to have been nothing other than God's grace, mercy, and love for me. I went through eight grades of school before my father made me drop out and would not allow me to enter high school. I was 15 years old by this time and was home all the time. This would prove to be a very bad situation for me. I had no other person in my life except my dad, and by the time I was 16, my life would take the most unbelievable and horrid turn. For the next three years, I would be far away from home and just trying to stay alive!

The terror truly started three years before I was 16. I remember the night very clearly. I was 13 years old. We had a small black-and-white TV, which was not allowed in the Mennonite church at the time. Dad got one anyway just to watch the news. He was denied membership at church because of this decision, though it did not seem to faze him. Dad and a few of my sisters were watching TV on this particular evening. It did not happen very often because life was so busy on the farm. I was very tired and fell asleep on the sofa. I awoke with Dad undressing me. Everyone else had gone to bed. This is still painful for me to write, so I will not go into detail. He had his hand on my mouth. He whispered in my ear to be quiet. I was raped that night and my entire life was changed forever. I had no choice in the matter. I tell young people today what a blessing it is to decide with whom and when you first have sex. I grieve having never had that. My innocence was violently and painfully taken away from me as a young child of 13 years! I'd like to think it would not have been as bad from a stranger or a criminal rapist. I cannot know the agony of those who've experienced it, but to have my own father betraying me in this way is still hard to believe. Even harder to fathom is that from that time on it would occur every night at 2 a.m. in my own bed for the next three years.

Another very sad fact is my mother knew and did nothing to protect me or stop him. I do remember a few times she tried by yelling at him to stop it. He made short work of that by slamming her against the wall. My Mom, fearing for her own life did not try to stop him after that. My sister was sleeping right next to me, in the same double bed, terrified and pretending to be asleep. She and I talk about it today still as we continue the lifelong healing process.

I have finally accepted the fact that it will take my whole lifetime to heal because of how long and severe it was. At the time of this writing, I am 61 years old. I am feeling so proud and awed at this strong young woman I am writing about now 48 years later. I know her. Where and how did she find the strength to survive such a horrible nightmare night after miserable night? She still had to get up at 4 a.m. to milk the cows. She still had to go to school. I have never known a more courageous little girl. Today when I get discouraged or depressed, I think of her. She motivates me to go on living joyfully and with a thankful heart. If she can do it, I can too. She is me! I am she! We are united as one.

Motivations for sharing my story

I want to honor her by telling you her story. Thus, I have just revealed to you one of the purposes of this book. I am giving God the glory also for my survival because I do not believe I would have made it without God's love, protection, and strength. I want to help other children and adults who have been victimized. I will go into detail later about the healing process. All I want to say here to those of you who have been a victim is that it is not your fault! You were a child and true victim. There was nothing you did to deserve it and nothing you could have done to stop it. Hear me clearly on this one. This is the number one rule of recovery: to accept that it was **not** your fault and there was **nothing** you could do to stop or prevent it!

I was so abused and traumatized that I never thought it could get any worse. In fact, I finally told someone what was going on. In light of this, I believed my freedom was just around the corner. Surely she would come and get me. She did come and get me, but we went to a counselor who was not helpful. All he told me to do was say, "No, I do not want to be raped anymore." He said, if that did not work, try throwing a shoe at him. This would have been between 1962 and 1964 in a very backward rural agricultural area, where such things were not handled well.

So I was taken back home and left. In retaliation against the person who took me to counseling, Dad let the air out of her tires. He also verbally threatened her if she ever came and took me anywhere again. Today, looking back, it shows how uneducated even so-called "professionals" were when it came to incest. This is when my dad had a feeling he was going to lose control, get caught, and lose me. I had just turned 16 when my dad came up with a plan to keep me all to himself. One day my Dad told me to get into the car with him. He told me we were going for groceries. What he did, however, was to literally kidnap me and kept driving. I had no idea where we were headed and I had a panic attack. I could barely breathe. I begged him to take me home. He reacted with angry words and threats that I had never heard before, and I was terrified and shut up.

He told me he would kill my mother or one of my sisters if I did not listen to his every command. Of course, this shock-and-fear tactic worked well. We rode in silence for the next two hours. I convinced him I needed to go to the bathroom. By that time I knew where we were headed. Some years earlier, Dad had bought a farm in New York State. Also he got a standalone house in the middle of nowhere. The farm was rented out. He also had a boat up there. He had taken my sisters and me up there a couple of times through the years. It had never been longer than a weekend. Now we were heading there alone. I was terrified not knowing what lay ahead, but fearing the worst based on my nightly 2 a.m. rape attacks. I felt sick and thought I might throw up. I somehow avoided it knowing that it would anger my dad and I did not want to incense him further, given this outburst of rage and the horrid threats to my mother and sisters. I felt very small and totally under his control. I also had other feelings for the first time as we rode in silence. I was aware of hate and anger. I knew that this would last longer than a weekend, but at the time I could never have acknowledged that this last stage of horrible abuse would be a little over two years. Then something happened that set in motion a chain of events that would end up with me planning a daring escape.

Looking back, I realize my dad was very violent a lot of the time. It was like walking on eggshells. We never knew what would set him off. I do remember something as little as not being able to find the car keys could trigger his rage. He would call my mom really bad things. Most of it is really too repugnant to write here in this book. He was also guilty of domestic violence toward my mother. I remember one case clearly when I was about seven. My mom was eight months pregnant with her ninth child. He flew into a rage against her for something. I do not have a memory of what it was about. I am clear, however, about the horrible result of his attack. He grabbed her, shoved her out of the house, onto the front porch, and locked the door. It was wintertime and cold outside. I remember also there was snow on the ground. She, of course, was not dressed for the cold.

So she knocked on the door and called out to him to let her in. What I witnessed next still sends chills through me as I write it down today. My dad opened the door, and I thought he was going to let her in. That is not what happened. He screamed at her, literally picked her up in his rage, and threw her down the steps. She lay in the snow, crying from pain and begging for help. I tried to go to her, but Dad would not let me.

"Leave her alone to learn her lesson," he said.

I can only stand in awe again at this brave little seven-year-old girl and what she managed to do as she was torn between love for her mother and fear of her father's rage.

There was mass confusion as the other children were crying. Dad was distracted from me for a minute. We had no phone in the house. I ran out the back door with just the clothes on my back, no shoes or coat, and never looked back. The nearest neighbor's house was where I headed. It was a quarter of a mile away. I hoped they were home, or my dad would kill me when I was discovered missing. They were home and called for an ambulance. I ran for home at that point. I was there when the ambulance came. It turned out my mother had a broken leg but the baby was not harmed. Three weeks later, she gave birth to my sister Darlene with a cast still on her leg. Of course, the real story of what happened was never told to the EMTs. We knew better than that. Our lives depended on backing up my dad when he told them she slipped and fell down the steps. We all told the same version. I believe the neighbors suspected abuse. Someone had called Child Protective Services and they came to investigate. We were all questioned, but no way was anyone going to tell the truth. All us kids looked healthy and well-fed and had no complaints. So, because of lack of evidence of abuse, the case was closed.

Year 1967

Now let's go back to the long, lonely trip to New York at age 16. The house in New York had bars on all the windows. I do not know why. Perhaps it had been a bank in the past. It was very odd-looking for a house, in my opinion. The only way in and out was with a key, so he could use it as a jail. That is what it became for me for the next two and a half years. That house was small, somewhere in a very country setting. I don't remember many details of my surroundings in this place. I think the closest big city was Buffalo. I never went anywhere so I don't know where I really was. My dad went home for several days at a time. He locked me up and left. No phone, no TV, just me. I did have some canned food—junk stuff like potato chips and pretzels. Those times were at least peaceful, as I was not being raped every night. I knew, though, that he would not be gone long. I dreaded his return.

As I reflect on this part of my life and write, I still have trouble understanding why help did not come. Where did my family think I was? Did they know? Was my mom just glad he was away from her and she was safe? We had a church. Why did the pastor not seek out my disappearance? I never did get those questions answered. I can only guess that my dad had everyone in the community fooled. And those at home and in the family were afraid of what he would do if confronted. His denial was believed. I say "denial" because I cannot fathom that anyone did not know. They had to! I was gone for too long.

Anyway, as I entered my 17th and 18th year, I began to change. I was getting stronger, older, and very angry at his abuse. Against my better judgment, the anger won and I began to hit him, kick, scream, and fight back. Most times he would just back off for a while and after I calmed down go for it again. He never completely gave up and let one night go by without rape.

This made me even more enraged. I fought him off for hours trying to go all night, but he always got his way. I did not know it at the time how much danger this behavior was putting me in. I was just so tired of it, but what happened one night changed my approach. I was saying no and he just snapped and flew into a rage that I had never seen before. I can say I thought my life was over. He put his hands around my neck and was strangling me. I had not experienced anything like this before. All I knew was that I could not breathe and this was it. I would be in heaven soon. I was fighting for my life! Then one of the many miracles of my life happened. I heard a voice very clear whisper in my ear:

"You cannot come to heaven yet. I have work for you to do. Just relax."

I believe to this day it was an angel or Jesus. The voice was so soothing and compelling that I did just that. I totally went limp and relaxed. In the next second, my dad just let go. I firmly believe my life was spared to spread the good news that Jesus is the way, the truth, and the life. I want to spend the rest of my life for him. He is my Savior, Lord, the best father and healer that I could ever have.

It was several months after my near-death experience that I woke up sick. I threw up and had trouble eating breakfast. It was not long before I learned the unthinkable had happened. I was pregnant with my dad's child! I was completely devastated! I cried out to God as never before. I could not believe my life had just been saved for this. This was absolutely senseless! I screamed. Now I really began to wish I had died. My life was completely ruined. However, God had something else in mind. With the benefit of hindsight, this was the turning point that led me to my deliverance. This final straw, becoming pregnant from my rapist father, turned out to be the best thing that could have happened to shock me into action.

My father denied that the baby was his, but that was beside the point. I knew it was. He knew it was! I had not been with anyone else. I could not comprehend giving birth to my dad's child. I'd been told about incest and how terrible the offspring often turned out. I was convinced that the baby might have a birth defect and not even be right mentally. I just wanted to get rid of it, and the shame of my father's child inside me, as soon as possible. My dad agreed to an abortion if I told them it was my boyfriend's baby. I said okay. The year was 1971. I was two days away from my 19th birthday. New York State was the first and only state with legalized abortion at that time. Through Planned Parenthood, it was arranged at a local hospital, with all false and made-up information that I created to heed my father's demands. Nothing real was used at all. This amazes me today for some reason how that was possible, but it happened. It was during this time of interacting with doctors, nurses, and social workers that I had an epiphany. It felt like an extremely bright light bulb flashed on in my head. The insight was something like a clear command inside of me.

Get away from him now! There is no rescue coming! Do whatever it takes but do it. He is planning on keeping you with him for the rest of your life."

A plan took shape in the form of many lies and promises to him that I had no intention of keeping. I told him that I missed my sisters and wanted to see them. I had not been home for almost three years. Of course, his first sentence was:

"No, because you will not come up here with me again."

I, however, promised him that I would. I told him I really liked it here. I said I enjoyed his company and would miss him if anything changed. Another miracle was about to unfold, as he believed me. I stayed calm and matter-of-fact as we headed home without my things, which reassured him I was returning. I was so glad to be home and see everyone. The first night I went to bed. I had no intention, however, of falling asleep. I waited and waited, watched the clock. A little after midnight with everyone asleep, I just simply got out of bed, walked out the door, and never looked back. At the neighbor's house I called 911. The police came and I told them to take me to my pastor's house. They had a rude awakening but took me in. I explained everything to them that night. In the morning, someone would show up at my home and tell my dad that I was at a safe place and would not be coming home.

It was my first taste of empowerment to move out of a victim role and into a brand-new life. I had no clue back then how seriously I had been wounded. I stayed with my pastor and his wife for about three months. Then they found a foster home for me to go to. They were loving people, and I did well there. They owned a bakery, where I worked making pies and sticky buns for restaurants. They also went to market every weekend and sold meats, cheese, and other deli items. I worked there, getting up at 3 a.m. for the long drive. The days were long and it was hard work, but I enjoyed it. I stayed with this family for about two years. I saw my dad maybe twice during that time with supervised visits. We did not talk much; he just said he wanted to see me and to know that I was okay. I told him I was and that was about the extent of my relationship with him until many years later. The only thing I remember during that period of my life was feeling homesick for my family, my sisters and brothers, and crying some.

I was 22 years old and getting restless where I was. I missed my sisters. I really do not remember whether I thought about my mom or not. It seems strange to me now looking back. My sister closest in age to me was 19 years old at the time and desperately wanting out of the home situation. I got word from her that things had not gotten any better. My dad was raging on. We decided to get a place together. The ideal place turned up in the form of a finished basement. A family with four children lived upstairs. We really liked it there, and I was glad my sister was out also.

We both found jobs at a nearby nursing home as aides. I also found work as a waitress. One day when I was working, this skinny Amish boy came in. He never left a tip and ate a huge breakfast. No one wanted to wait on him, so I always volunteered. He made calls from the phone booth for hours and then came in to eat. We always wondered what he did in the phone booth for so long. I found out later that the Amish are not allowed to have phones in their homes. He was calling customers and making other business calls. I would see him again when the famous flood of 1972, due to Hurricane Agnes, hit Lancaster County. He was cleaning up outside, and I cleaned mud off windows on the inside. He looked up at me, waved, and smiled. I smiled and waved back. I was flattered and thought he was kind of cute, but he was Amish, and I knew they did not date outside of their religious sect. I did not give it much thought after that.

I had been attending a charismatic church in the area for a few months. I was making friends and liked it. I started singing and working in the nursery. One Sunday morning, as I was leaving church, I met that Amish guy again. This time he looked different. He was not dressed in his Amish clothes. This drew my attention. He was very handsome and obviously had gone out of his way to make sure I noticed him. He said he was leaving the Amish and coming to this church. Now he had my total attention. But I'm getting ahead of myself.

3

Another Blow—Does It Never End?

The call came while I was at work. The year was 1999. This was not just any call. This was one that no one wants to get. It was a family member telling me, "We lost Darlene today." At first the way she said it had me confused. Then she just told me outright that Darlene was dead. Darlene, my second youngest sister, had committed suicide. This was to be the second child in our family to commit suicide.

I was grief-stricken. There were six of us girls. We all sang together on occasion. One of the many sad things about her death was that we never sang together again after that. She was our alto. She was gifted with just being able to hear the harmony, which the rest of us were not always successful at. She left behind her husband and three beautiful, devastated children, one of whom found her. Thirteen years later, that now adult child who found his dead mother is still struggling with the effects. She had just turned 40 years old. Through the years, we would find out that basically she was a victim of unresolved childhood pain. Her pain wanted to burst out so she could be healed. But she resisted and harbored the pain through denial, fearing its power, until death was the only release she could figure out. Her therapist told us denial killed her. I wish that my sister would have lived longer. As I learned to deal with childhood pain, perhaps I could have helped her, but it was not to be.

Denial killed my sister. I write this to help each of you realize the risk of keeping pain like this bottled up inside. Find someone to talk to. Work it out! Do **not** live in denial. The cost is too high!

4

Letting Love In

Remember the Amish boy a few pages back? The boy who left the Amish way and I met again after we exchanged smiles in the cleanup of the 1972 flood? Remember how I'd met him at a charismatic church and he'd caught my eye?

Dan and I started dating and got married in 1976, when I was 25 years old. That is the story with which I opened this story line. Later, after we were married, he told me he fell in love with me at the flood scene when he waved and smiled at me. He knew I was the one he would marry.

When we got married, his parents gave us an acre of land from their farm to build a house on. It took us several years to save up, but we finally built a brick rancher in 1980. It had a big bay window out front overlooking trees, and flowers bloomed in the garden. There was open farmland all around us, and I could see the Amish planting corn and plowing fields. It was so peaceful and quiet because they farm with horses; no noises from tractors.

By 1979 I had been married three years. Dan worked long hours getting his business started and making money. He was very driven and really enjoyed what he did.

The business was called Elite Genetics. Dan served as a middleman dealing with farmers who wanted to breed their cows to the best bulls in order for them to produce more milk. It was a new concept back then. The process was not to have just one bull run with the herd. Each cow and bull was studied, and they were matched up to produce the best milk yield possible. His business was a huge success. As a young Amish boy growing up on a farm and milking cows, he became interested in learning this concept. We had a home office. I helped him with answering the phones and doing paperwork. The business grew very quickly, with customers all over the United States. In the years to come, it would expand to include other countries as well. For all practical outward purposes, our life was good and going well.

5

Adventures, Elite Genetics, and Service

Dan came home one day excited with what he considered great news. I, however, was a bit horrified when he told me he bought a pot-bellied pig for $10,000. I did calm down a little when he explained that she was pregnant with 10 babies. He was counting the money to be made already in his head. With his research on how popular these new pets were becoming, he figured each baby could be sold for around $5,000 each. I was stunned! That was $50,000 gross, $40,000 in net profit. I was not so positive that someone would pay that much for a pet pig. As it turned out, this was the first of many business deals that my husband would make. Eventually, I freaked out less and began to trust his business sense. The pig did have 10 healthy babies, and he did get all of $5,000 for each one. Even Channel 8, the local news station, came out and did a story on these exotic pets. Toward the end of this stage, we had a pet pig, Petra, in the house for almost a year. He was from a litter born too soon and was the only survivor. I fed him every two hours. He was so tiny and kept under a heat lamp.

This pet became very loving and lay on the sofa asleep while we watched TV. He used a litter box like a cat and was very easy to train.

The pot-bellied pig rage did not last long, and eventually they became worthless. By this time, my husband was on to the next new money-making venture. So when he came home with a camel that he had bought for $7,000. I was not surprised. This camel was sold to Sight and Sound, a local theater, to be used in their shows. Then there were the ostriches and emus. A market developed for a while in Texas for ostrich meat. This too phased out in time.

My husband was good at what he did and was in each venture only for a short time. He scooped the cream off the top and moved on. He explained it to me in terms of surfing. I catch the big wave and ride on top of it all the way to the beach. When that wave is done, it's done, and you have to go on to the next one. If you try to keep riding the same wave, you lose. Others at times saw how much money he was making in Elite Genetics and tried to get in on it. But it was too late for them—the wave was already on the shore.

Dan believed, and I did also, that God gave him this special gift to make money. We gave at least 50 percent away to missions. His main motivation was to give. We lived a modest lifestyle. We were truly rich and blessed. Dan served as mission's director for a large church in the area. He designed and built seven churches in Jamaica. With his unique knowledge, the churches doubled as a storm shelter. I traveled with him several times as did our daughter Jennifer. This was her foundation for what she does now in full-time missions. When she was only two or three years old, she sang in a church service in Jamaica. An attendance of over a thousand people did not faze her. She was bold and still is. God gave her a lot of her father's gifts to help others.

A Shadow Within

As I have said before, on the outside my life and marriage to Dan were good. Inside my heart, however, was a different story. The secret that I kept to myself on my wedding day would manifest as an uncontrollable demon of torment in my marriage. The unresolved terror of my wretched abusive childhood experiences could no longer be stuffed down. Normal "relations" in marriage brought everything back to the surface, and what I thought was long gone had only gained intensity lying in the bank of self-deceit and denial.

I began to compare my husband to the fantasy of my first lost love. That, combined with all those years of unresolved grief and horror, made me very unhappy and lonely. I became a nag. At the time, I really was not aware that "the problem" in my marriage was part of my root problem of abuse, not a major defect in my husband. Back then, he was the enemy, and it was he keeping me from being happy and content in life. For him, life was rosy and he was having a blast. He began to travel a lot on business and would be gone for up to several weeks at a time. This certainly did not help matters at all for me. He totally did not understand why I complained so much. He did try his best to help by giving me the credit card and sending me out shopping. This was only a temporary fix, but it worked for awhile. I filled my closet with beautiful clothes and shoes. I bought clothes and toys for my daughter also. I hated cooking, and he did not like what I made. My husband fixed this by eating out a lot.

He was basically a good man and tried to do his best to make me happy. Of course, the real problems had to do with me not sharing my past tortured life with him and my own unresolved damage from a life of sexual abuse! He had no clue how wounded and broken I really was. *Neither did I.* We kept going, day to day, the best we could. By the end of 1981, however, I was seriously depressed and extremely lonely. I wish then that I had had the wisdom of hindsight and could have known what was driving me and all the negative emotions. All I knew was to find some way to get relief from the pain. None of it was thought out beforehand. The series of events that would unfold would lead me on a very dangerous journey and into another nightmare of gigantic proportions.

I stepped out into the night. It was early fall. The weather was beautiful, and a nearly full moon was visible in the clear sky. I felt rotten on the inside, though. That feeling was totally appropriate, because, as the Eagles' song puts it, I was "headed for the cheatin' side of town."

I ended up far from town, however. I was with someone, and we parked beside a body of water with a pier to walk out on. We spent most of the night there. That is about all I remember. It was an incredibly dangerous position to have put myself in. I did not know him very well, and I easily could have been harmed or murdered that night.

Looking back on this part of my life is very difficult for me. I am not going into more detail than is needed to share my story. The choices I made for the next year after that night still remain some of the worst choices in my life.

These damaging actions were of my own making and to this day still confound and rip at me. This is part of my motivation to write this down and get it out to others who have been abused. The abuse is like runners of some vine, seeking out cracks and chinks, and burrowing deep into our subconscious until they've taken over much of our thoughts and actions—things we do not understand, see, or seem to have any way to control—but our only hope is to ferret them out, get them into the light of day, and start to deal with them, in order to start to weed them out and regain control of our life.

I was just getting a quick fix and a high as if on some drug. I would feel loved and pain-free for awhile. The trouble was, as with any drug of choice, it did not last. Reality would raise its ugly head soon after, and I would come crashing down, feeling miserable and worse than before. Then I would need another fix, and it would start all over again. I was a massive train wreck and I knew it. I just didn't know why!

For the first time in my adult life, I wanted to die. The only thing that kept me from ending my own life, as two of my siblings had done, was my beautiful, innocent three-year-old daughter. She was my reason to stay vertical on the planet. I was stubborn enough not to want anyone else raising her. I had to stay sane and alive for her.

For her sake, I quit cold turkey with the cheating. What I could not stop, though, was the loneliness, pain, depression, and despair. Looking back, I understand now that my bad feelings were those of the powerless, little abused girl-child trying to speak, feel, and get a voice after all these years. The past was trying to break through so that I could be healed, but I had no idea at the time that that was what was happening, so I fought it.

You see, whenever I did allow myself to remember my past, I recalled the atrocities of my past as a factual event in my life, but I had no emotional feelings about them whatsoever. Much later I learned that in order to heal from those atrocities, I have to feel.

HEAR ME:

Do **not** let the fear of experiencing the pain (of what you denied) prevent you from taking that step. It is worth it! The pain you cause yourself by unresolved suffering may and usually will be **greater** than whatever pain you have to face to get well and find healing.

Back then I assumed that I was healed from all that happened. I did not feel the pain, because of my denial. After all, I had zero feelings about it. It was just a fact, as if I had read it in a newspaper. I truly believed that I must have been healed because it did not have any emotional hold on me. What a lie!

Of course, what other conclusion could I have come to? My memories having no pain attached to them now made sense, for I had disassociated myself from my feelings in order to survive the anguish. I can certainly see why I made no connection between the pain in my marriage and my resulting sexual acting out and my torrid past. Meanwhile, the present got worse! I ended up telling my husband that I had been cheating on him for about a year when he was away traveling on business. I spent the next ten years begging him to love me and trust me again. I still did not recognize or deal with the pain or share the cause of it with Dan, because I had no clue it was the root of all evil in my life. It remained only this **fact** that had occurred but seemingly had no emotional connection to my present turmoil. I never shared it or allowed him to learn about it.

He, however, found it impossible to forgive me. So we both became stuck with no solutions in sight. By 1984 my husband was seriously depressed due to money problems from some business reversals and, I am sure, our marriage issues.

We experienced one bright spot in 1984, when I gave birth to our second daughter. She was the light in the darkness. Dan was crazy in love with his baby girl. We named her Angela Dawn—our angel and new beginnings. We wished and hoped that this would be a new beginning for us. I thought maybe our marriage could still be saved. Toward that end, I got in therapy five years later, around 1989.

Two years after that, it became clear that our marriage was over. I had learned a lot, but it was too late. I blame mostly myself for the marriage failure because of the cheating. I did work hard on forgiving myself and moving on. So it was a very sad day in 1991 when I moved out with our two precious girls and started over in an apartment. Dan was a very good father and continued to be in their lives. He faithfully paid child support without having to involve the courts. What a blessing that was! We never used our children as pawns. We gave them permission to love both parents. I also remember continually reassuring them it was not their fault. Dan took them on trips together and did many fun things with and for them. He really loved his daughters. His loving nicknames for them were Joy and Dawn, their middle names. It is so sweet to treasure those memories today.

In 1998 I went into therapy because of the pain my failed marriage was causing me. I was 38 years old, and at this point I still had no emotional feelings associated with the memories of what I went through in childhood. I still assumed that when I got away from my dad, I was fine. I was in denial and did not even know it. Well, how could I have ever known anything without any emotion associated with the memories?

As it turned out, I could not begin to work on the pain of the past without the trigger of present pain. I was going to learn and unlearn many things over the coming years. It amazes me today at 61 years of age how that works. I did not know that the facts alone without the feelings attached to them would bring no healing. Without feeling them, I had no hope of healing. I also did not know that I needed to heal. I'd learned so well to **block everything**, in order to cope with the terrific horror, that I didn't even know I had anything requiring healing. It was all some big mysterious blur in my mind I could not feel or understand. How could I have known the heroic young girl that I had been was so wounded? I needed to get to know her. As yet she was a stranger. She had very dysfunctional behaviors, ways of thinking, and a belief system that, as a child abuse victim, had kept her alive. I had very low self-esteem and tapes playing in my head that turned out to be mostly lies. In today's language, in might be better understood as baggage, and lots of it.

Little Ruthie

As an adult, I needed to be a safe and loving parent to Little Ruthie (me as a child) so she could heal. I needed to reclaim my lost and stolen childhood. Some of this healing included going to the park with my children and being a child with them. I would swing on the swings beside them, laughing and screaming with glee as we went higher and higher. I also went down the sliding board with them. We had so much fun together. I would tell my girls that Little Ruthie wants to come out and play. As I was the parent I never had to my two girls, I joined them in recapturing my own lost childhood and started the long road to healing.

They still remember those times when we talk today. I surrounded myself with little children. I experienced their innocence. I did what they did. I bought a coloring book. I got down on the floor by myself many times with my crayons and colored. I started a journal and wrote to Little Ruthie. I became her loving parent. I told my Little Ruthie how much I loved her and that nothing my dad had done to her was in any way her fault. I got out the pictures I had when I was little. I saw how beautiful she was. I learned to stop hating her and accept her, and to start to accept God's grace. I saw that Little Ruthie was strong and courageous. She was a survivor and endured untold torment of body, soul, and spirit. Against incredible odds, this child had done whatever she could to stay alive. I was in awe and inspired by her as I continued to heal.

This included a long grieving process once I realized how much I had lost and how much my dad had taken from me. Some of that damage I will surely take with me to my grave. I learned that there was still a high price that I would have to pay, even though it was not my fault, for there was much pain to endure to start the healing and having a whole and complete life after my history of abuse.

A big part of the healing process is to take responsibility to heal for myself as an adult, no matter what it takes. It was all up to me now. Yes, my father bears all the blame for what he did to me as a child and into my young adulthood. The big thing that I was learning in therapy was that I cannot continue to blame him for my mistakes and failures as an adult, including my marriage. That was the part of taking responsibility for my own choices, regardless of the circumstances that led me to those choices.

What? But it *was* his entire fault—everything! It all sounded so unfair to me. The thing about it was that it *was* unfair. The nature of life itself on this earth is not fair. It never will be. This is one of the first things that I was able to teach my daughters as I healed. They would fuss and complain about those lessons, but today they thank me for it. Facing life with "realistic expectations" is a big part of being healthy. Today in 2012, as I write this, Jennifer is a healthy 38-year-old young woman who has just gotten married. Her new husband is a wonderful young Christian man. He is the kind of man that I would have wanted for a husband and for my daughters. It brings me great joy to see how she is so happy in life and doing well. She is in full-time ministry helping others through YWAM (Youth with a Mission) in California. My baby Angela is also doing well. I am so proud of her. She and her boyfriend live in Pennsylvania. She has a master's degree and works as a school psychologist.

The Breakthrough

It only took one major, horrific memory to break through my denial, my subconscious, and into the light of day. Denial was impossible afterward. All those years of repressed feelings and unemotional "facts" started to be chiseled away.

It all came about when I had spent about five months in therapy. The year was 1989. I was 38 years old and still married to Dan. I was beginning to trust my therapist and feel safe. I was letting down my guard. She started asking me a lot about my childhood. I did tell her a lot of facts from my head, as I had done many times before with other people. Somehow, over time, as I told my story to her over and over again, something was changing. I felt more and more *uncomfortable*. I did not understand what was happening. That was the start of my feelings about my tortured past beginning to stir within me. At that moment, I had a premonition that something *huge* was about to happen.

When I got home from therapy that particular night, I was tired and flopped down on the sofa to rest, but I did not fall asleep. I just closed my eyes and saw a vision, a flashback of me as a little four-year-old girl. I was standing in the dining room screaming at my dad to stop. The scene I was seeing was of my mother lying on the floor. My dad was sitting on her waist, hitting her in the face, head, arms, whatever was available. I saw myself run to him and try to pull him off my mother. He yelled at me to leave him alone, and with one huge swing of his hand, he hit me away and I flew across the room to land on the floor in a crying heap under the dining room window. It was so vivid, dark, and frightening that I can still see it clearly in my mind today. The horrible pain and fear that little girl experienced at that time, and many, many times thereafter, are unexplainable. I had one more memory of my mother from when I was around five years old. She was lying in bed crying. I asked her why she was crying. She said because Daddy hurt her.

I said, "Why did Daddy hurt you?"

She replied, "His head does not work right. There is something wrong with it."

These were two very vivid memories that surfaced involving my mother. The rest of the memories that came through were of my dad's abuse. That was the beginning of one horrible scene after another over a period of five years until they stopped. The pain of grief, loss, and trauma from those suppressed memories was nearly unbearable. I felt like experiencing one more memory would take my breath away and surely I would die.

I don't share this to frighten you away from confronting your own demons, but to be honest in knowing it is not a free ride. The end is worth the drama and trauma, but the trick is to be in a solid counseling situation or seek one immediately when the memories start to respond in "living color and 3D"!

My good news is that I had a skilled therapist who helped guide me through the pain and reliving those suppressed memories. She taught me how to take slow deep breaths, like a woman with labor pains giving birth. She suggested I buy a stuffed animal to hold onto when in pain. I bought a soft, lovable puppy that I took with me to therapy and used at home when the pain would naturally wash over me. Slowly, healing began to creep in. I could feel the lessening of the anguish. I was seeing an end of the horror. I began to relax, thinking it was over when I was taken off-guard with another emotion even more powerful and dangerous.

Enter the devil's revenge: ***ANGER***!

I finally realized how badly I had been hurt and damaged by the abuse. It would take the rest of my life to recover. When it all started to come into focus, the anger was actually more like rage. It was murderous rage. I really felt capable of killing my dad. I wanted to, but again, my therapist kept me grounded. She said something I have never forgotten to this day:

"The best revenge is to live well."

She would ask me: "How well would you live if you killed him and went to jail?" This registered with me and made sense, even through it was extremely difficult to let go of the rage once it roared up into my consciousness. I put my mind and heart to the task of working through my rage. At my therapist's suggestion, I furiously wrote all my feelings down in a letter to my father.

I read it and reread it. Then I tore it up and did it again. I do not remember how many times I repeated this, but it really helped me channel my anger and rage. Another exercise I did was also powerful. I went to the basement, taking a chair with me. I set it out in front of me and imagined my dad sitting in it. I took a pillow, screamed at him, and beat him to death until I was exhausted. I did this many times when the rage wanted to overtake me. There is no one-size-fits-all when it comes to the healing process. Each of us will need to find our own release. God never intended for a child to be so treated, but He protected me . . . and my gratitude demanded that I not violate yet another of His commandments and commit murder.

Everyone is different and has their own time and way. The last stage for me was dealing with shame and feeling dirty. As the memories surfaced and became so vivid, I remember obsessively taking showers over and over again, trying to feel clean. Even though the shame clearly belonged to my father, this was very hard for me to let go of. Rape is rape . . . incest rape by a parent or family member may have other power, but shame is often a companion to the victim in rape, and the victim must battle back against those feelings. Maybe some of the struggle was due to the fact that I was 19 years old before I managed to get away from that constant abuse that lasted for so many years. As I continued with my great therapist, I learned about brainwashing, dependency issues, and many other things that go with abuse. She explained a lot of things to me. One statement she made that helped me the most was, "You got away from him as soon as you could. If you were capable of getting away sooner, you would have."

When abuse is as severe and extends over many years as mine did, she told me she was amazed I stayed alive, much less got away in the end, the way I did. She informed me that my abuse experience was the worst she had ever come across in over 25 years of practice. She told me that she admired me and what I had accomplished. This helped me to accept myself. I learned to love the strong young woman that I was.

Facing the Foe

After a lot of hard work and five years of good therapy, I was getting ready to face my dad in person. I had no idea how he would respond. I was 43 years old, and we had never talked about it. Now it was time.

I drove down to the farm one day to meet my father. I took a trusted friend with me for support and for safety (remember my dad's frequent rage and physical outbursts). I had achieved a lot in recovery, but I was still very anxious and afraid. I just *knew* I needed to confront him. I had nothing written down, nor did I have a script. I had basically one question. *Why?* I really envisioned him being angry and defensive, giving endless excuses, and maybe even denying that it ever happened. I tried to prepare for anything. What happened in reality, though, was not anything like what I had tried to get ready for. I was still a little angry when I asked why.

He simply said, "I don't know."

I was about to start an argument from that statement when he continued.

He added, "But what I do know is that I have no excuse to give you. It should never have happened no matter what. I am so sorry. Will you forgive me?"

I was speechless. My mouth was hanging open but no words were coming out. I looked at my friend for help, but she was as frozen in time as me. I got my voice in a few minutes and mumbled something like "I guess so . . ."

Then I thanked him for meeting with me and quickly left. I was very anxious and uncomfortable. Looking back, this was really a great response, perhaps even a "God-incidence" (not coincidence), and helped me in the long run with my journey of true healing and forgiveness.

In the moment, however, on the way home, I realized that I had *wanted* an argument. I had wanted to vent on him. In spite of the "no revenge policy," I had wanted *some revenge* that day. None of that happened, and I hate to say it, but I was disappointed. The bottom line was that I was not ready to forgive. Oh, I knew I would in the end, but not like that. Not at the first meeting. Not without at least a fight. I found myself angry again. I found out that I would need to do some more work. Full forgiveness did come, but not until after many more years of my own hard work and healing.

I had more meetings with my father. In these meetings, my heart was better prepared to extend true forgiveness to him. I will never forget the day when I was able to look him in the eye and say those powerful, difficult words: "I forgive you."

The choice to forgive is an ongoing process. Whenever tempted to take it back, I renew my forgiveness again. I remind myself that I forgave him for me to be free. Not because he deserved it. Not because I felt like it. I never did feel like it. Forgiveness is not agreeing with the horrible acts that were done. Forgiveness is agreeing with God when he says that vengeance belongs to Him. He will repay. He is the ultimate judge, and the Bible says that every knee shall bow and every tongue will confess to Him. God forgave me the things I did wrong, gave me grace, and I'm called to reflect that to my worst enemy.

6
A Look Back
What Factors Were in Play?

What Makes a Parent an Abuser?

I wanted to share a little bit with you about my parents' background. I need to say upfront that their past does not in any way make okay what my dad did or my mother allowed. The only advantage for me in knowing their past is that it helped me to understand them, have compassion, and eventually forgive them for what they did to me. I have read many books about survivors of abuse. I began to notice a common theme running through most of them. It seemed to me that most people that were abusers had been abused themselves at some point in their lives, usually in childhood.

My mother came from a large family of 12 children. I was not able to get my mother to share her childhood with me. I can only guess from how her life unfolded and the struggles of her brothers and sisters. Mother recently passed away, after battling Alzheimer's, so I will never know. The fact that she was secretive, not sharing anything good or bad, makes me wonder what her childhood was like. I do get the feeling that there was abuse of some kind in her family. I do know that there were depression, two suicides, and other attempted suicides in my mother's immediate family. That tells me something about the mental health—or lack thereof—in her family. I wish I knew more about what happened, but as of today, no one still living is willing to talk. My mother's family, like my own, was involved in very fundamental rural church life, where much was ignored or swept under the rug.

My dad was a talker, on the other hand, and gave me a lot of information about his past. He came from a broken and abusive home. His mother was a prostitute prior to and *during* her marriage to my grandfather. She had six boys and really had no idea who their fathers were. My dad's father was an alcoholic and road walker. He walked the roads picking up soda cans, bottles, or whatever else he could find. The money he got for them and other odd jobs was spent on booze.

My grandparents got divorced when my father was young. He told me many times his mother would tie him up with rope to the kitchen table as a toddler and give him a bottle of (sour) milk while she went out. Often she would be gone all night, and he would cry himself to sleep with the kitchen floor as his bed. My heart ached for that little boy. He deserved better. When he was 15 years old, he ran away from home. He went to work in the fields and milking cows for a Mennonite farmer in the area. They took him to the Mennonite church they attended. That is where he met my mother. He was a true victim as a child. However, he stayed in denial, was totally unaware, and as a result, he did not heal and, as an adult, became the perpetrator. He victimized others and passed the abuse he himself had suffered along to the next generation. This to me is very, very sad! The Bible calls this the "generational curse." There is a great possibility that many generations of abuse occurred and were passed down before it got to me.

Generational Abuse and the Abuse Cycle

They say that history repeats itself. They also say that if we don't learn from history, we're destined to repeat it. Sayings abound from our forefathers like that. There is another saying that is relevant here: that the *sins of the father will be visited upon the children.* Depending on whom you talk to or what source you reference, you get different explanations regarding how the circle remains unbroken. Abuse fits all these sayings in one way or another.

Where does abuse start? Much research has been done on abuse, including bullying in schools, and one minister did his doctoral dissertation on the cycle of abuse in churches, no less! The theory is that unless the cycle is broken, abuse in a nuclear family is destined to be repeated and played out over and over again.

I've shared about my own sexual abuse as a child. I've shared what little I know about my father and his family. It is clear that there was some sort of abuse in his childhood.

It's not an excuse for those who abuse to say that they too were abused. Each generation has the responsibility and opportunity to end the cycle of abuse, but realistically speaking, if we look back at our parents, our grandparents and great-grandparents, and trace a cycle of abuse, there were very few options for counseling, intervention, or even protection until the latter part of the 20th century. And depending on the locale, those resources might still be very limited to help a person who had a childhood of abuse find help in healing and breaking that cycle of abuse.

The best defense is sometimes said to be a good offense. Hmmm . . . how can we use that saying in relationships and especially dating or marriage to avoid entanglement with an abusive person? Do abusers carry cards? No! Do they exhibit special characteristics or behaviors or dress certain ways so that we can recognize them in advance? No!

When we meet someone who seems nice, of either sex, and find them interesting, entertaining, joyful, smart, or attractive, would we be able to tell soon after that they came from an abusive background? Perhaps more of us than we think would not see the warning signs.

Friends I knew for several years, during the worst of my recovery time, never sensed that I had been abused. Even when I told some of them that I was abused as a child that was not very illuminating to them. You see, *abuse* is a term that has been used and even overused in society over the past 20 years to mean a spectrum of behaviors, from the hardcore sexual abuse, rape, and molestation I knew, to lesser degrees of intimidation, emotional and verbal harassment, condescension, and being screamed at daily.

I've met people who were verbally abused. They were screamed at every day, cursed, threatened, and put down, but were never hit, touched, or physically mistreated. Many said they'd rather have been beaten physically than to be verbally assaulted day in and day out for reasons that were beyond their comprehension.

Psychologists have case files full of notes, but to date, there are only global generalizations about abuse and that abused children often grow up to be abusers themselves.

Does that mean someone who was screamed at as a child will become verbally abusive? Or might they mutate into a hitter instead since they "wished" they'd been struck rather than constantly berated? Or might they be so damaged from the verbal abuse and so emotionally stilted that they cannot relate to the opposite sex and become a sexual abuser of children?

All that is seemingly known is that abuse seems to create more abuse. My father was certainly abused growing up in the environment he described. In the fundamentalist view, it is the man who was always right and unchallenged. Therefore, if his father was abused by a dictatorial father, then my grandfather's father was likely abusive as well. Generational abuse is not a Xerox copy of the one before and may mutate from being harsh, cold, withdrawn, and condescending to screaming or being physically abusive with regular beatings. All that is known at this point in time is that abuse is usually generational and repeats itself.

Earlier I suggested that perhaps a good defense is a better offense. What would that mean when sifting and sorting through individuals of the opposite sex to a person who has had an abusive past?

It takes two things to have abuse occur: First, the person who ends up a victim often has been through a situation in childhood or adolescence that has robbed them of their self-esteem so that they think being treated poorly is what they deserve or the best they can expect. With low self-worth, they can become more easily engulfed in an abusive situation. Second, the abuser has to have some experience with abuse in their own past to push them to be abusive. If you've been abused, which will *you* be? Victim or abuser?

The cycle of abuse, once started, can so easily be repeated over and over without anyone ever stopping to see what is happening. People, once hurt, tend to protect themselves with a good offense, or they become the victim and are a target for further abuse until that cycle is broken.

So how do those who have been abused prevent themselves from carrying forth the abuse to others, their own family members, children, or spouse?

I'll say this **again**: They need to throw off the denial and shame long enough to admit that there was abuse and **seek qualified counseling** to heal their own wounds and prevent them from becoming another victim due to their low self-esteem, to help them realize the risks associated with their past pushing them to be either a victim or an abuser, and to ensure that whatever mechanism they've used to get out of their own abusive past does not orient them to draw "first blood" as a prevention against abuse.

Acceptance and self-awareness of your past is your first line of a good offense. Then you need to seek out help in preventing that abuse from being replicated as a victim or abuser. Take the offensive against your own abusive past to ensure you don't fall prey to being a victim or becoming an abuser.

Second, heed the words "Take time to know him, it's not an overnight thing," as Jody Miller sang on her album *Will You Love Me Tomorrow*. In our society today, with instant everything and microwave meals, we want "instant" relationships. Why else would over 50 percent of marriages end in divorce? People are racing to fulfill a need that they do not yet understand and have not taken "time to know" a potential partner.

In the old days, people would "court." They would do things in mixed groups, spend evenings with someone at that person's family's home. They got to see "under the covers" a bit in those visits how the family interacted. If it was too plastic and perfect, alarm bells might go off and make one wonder "what's up with that?" Today, people move out of their nuclear family earlier, move off to college, and people only get to see the other person in isolation away from their nuclear family.

A good offense might be spending time with the family of someone who interests you . . . or at least, spend a good bit of time with them and their friends. Time spent when another person is in a relaxed atmosphere with people they've associated with for a long time, like family or old friends, often provides a comfort zone for otherwise covered behaviors to surface and show things that one-to-one dating under ideal conditions will never show.

A good "offense," then, is to "take time to know them"—and in a myriad of everyday life situations and with a wide variety of people—especially those with whom they would be most comfortable. Until recently I was unaware of how intense my fear has been in driving me to be "connected" to a man. Spending time with a person in whom you're interested may not be revealing if you do so with blinders on and are " bent to election" to accomplish a preordained goal regardless of the data that is put before you.

So the first step in preventing being abused as you were in your family of origin, when you move into a relationship or marriage, is to leave no stone unturned in your quest to identify how deeply you've been hurt and to expose your innermost beliefs about dating, relationships, and being alone or not alone. You also need to recognize the values you seek in a mate and what "life script" issues you have for what you think is acceptable and what is not when it comes to being partnered versus being alone.

Having this understanding, I have made it my life's mission to break the cycles of abuse in my own family, and it is my hope to educate others to do the same. The way to do this is first, to enter treatment and get healing.

As I moved from victim to survivor and overcame the abuse, the vision became clear. I knew how terrible being abused felt, so why would I ever want to pass that pain on to anyone else, much less my children and loved ones? Just the thought of it was so abhorrent that I probably went overboard in my decision never to abuse my children. I was determined not even to raise my voice to them or my husband. I can honestly say that for the most part I carried that promise out. I know I was not perfect, but my children do testify today that I was a great mom. They have in no way ever been abused. This encourages me and is one of the many miracles that I have witnessed. The curse, at least in my relationship with my nuclear family, is broken and will not be passed on to the next generation. In fact, all my sisters have done this also. They have happy, educated, well-adjusted children. Some have married well and have children of their own. I pray for them all the time. As far as I know, none of us has passed abuse to the next generation. I also believe God that none of the 20 grandchildren will ever divorce, let alone abuse.

7

Awesome God and Forgiveness

I am thinking of the Bible verse that says, "Now unto him that is able to do exceedingly, abundantly above all that we could ask or think" (Ephesians 3:20–21). I certainly see that happening in my family of origin today. My parents had 20 grandchildren and three great-grandchildren as I wrote the first edition of this book in 2012. My siblings and their offspring are all healthy and doing well. From the home that we grew up in to where we are today is a modern miracle, and a testament to God's mercy and grace as well. Without a relationship with Him, this would probably be a completely different story. In spite of all that was happening, we went to church every Sunday. I learned about Jesus and all the stories of the Bible. I memorized many verses in the Bible. Most of them I can still quote today. When I was 12 years old, I accepted Jesus in my heart as Lord and Savior. I remember praying and crying out to God for deliverance through my years of abuse. I believe this was my lifeline and hope as a young child. My mother prayed fervently also for all of her children. I believe God heard and answered her cries to Him. I still wish my mother would have done more to protect me. After having children of my own, I understand even less why she didn't. If my husband or anyone else was raping my daughters, I think I would just have to kill him in the act. I am not saying that that would be the right thing to do, but this is just how I feel. I learned not to try to understand my mother. In light of where she may have come from and the fundamentalist church world she lived in, she did the best she could. My father told me when he was taking me to New York and hiding me away for his sordid personal pleasures that if I ran away or told anyone, he would kill my mother and my sisters. I will never know how he may have threatened my mother with what he might do to me or to my siblings if she said anything, and she may have believed he would do those terrible things just as I believed he would harm my mother and sisters.

I have let it go and have forgiven her. I became able to love her and have a close relationship with her. Today I am so glad I did.

At the time I began writing this book, she was 88 years old and lived with my sister. She had dementia so bad that she cannot speak. I do believe she knew my Dad and her caregivers. She was bedridden and just existing, nothing but skin and bones. It was very difficult to see her, and I grieved because even though she was alive, she was dead. I do really miss her. I sometimes prayed for God to take her home. I released her to Him and let her go. I know God loves her and has His timing, not mine. My father was 89 years old and lived in a nursing home nearby. One of us children took him to see Mom almost every day. I saw that he had learned a lot in the past four years and was actually tender toward Mom and told her he loved her. I believe that was the first time ever that I had seen and witnessed this kind of behavior from him.

Seeing that has also helped to continue the healing process for us as a family. It was wonderful to see them have a few good years together before she drifted away from us through the clouds of dementia. They had been married for 65 years in 2012.

I am feeling so glad for this kind of closure. I realize that not everyone has had this opportunity for healing and closure. I am glad that the past is now behind me, and the future is whatever I want it to be. Life on this earth is short. When I first wrote this, I was now 61 years old, and it was time for me to search out what God desired of me. As a single woman I still wanted to be in a happy, Godly marriage. I was waiting on Him to see whether it was His will for this miracle to come about. I believed and still believe God "is able to do exceedingly, abundantly above all that we could ask or think" (Ephesians 3:20). It is very exciting at this point in my life to see what God will do. I still look forward to retirement, singing again, and being involved in ministry wherever He calls me.

As I write and reflect on the past, some present issues assert themselves. That is a good thing, because then they can be worked on. Also, a good book that I have, called *Shame Lifter* by Marilyn Hontz, is very insightful on this subject. I am going to read it again and again if I need to. None of us will ever be finished learning and growing. This is especially true of me, considering my past. Right now, I am struggling with shame because of being married and divorced three times. I have been thinking about some refresher therapy to help rid myself of this feeling. My third divorce was final on October 1, 2010. After that I had a desire to date again. But before I could do that, my shame had to go. I need to be able to forgive myself. I have to see me as God sees me. Simply forgiven! "As far as the east is from the west, so far has He removed our transgressions from us" (Psalm 103:12). So if I hold onto shame and keep talking to God about things that are forgiven, He says, "I don't remember. I do not know what you are talking about, because I forgot."

When I see it this way, I start to chuckle, because I am so hard on myself. Why do we tend to make our own struggles so much more difficult than they have to be? God's truth is simple if I would just believe what He says. I am worthy and deserving of love because of him taking my sins and failures on the cross. I am free of condemnation. What am I afraid of? Probably rejection by someone I am dating or wanting to date. In reality the thing that usually happens is that I reject myself first from the inside out. I first reject myself if I am feeling shameful, however subconscious that is. This then needs to be brought to a conscious level so it can be dealt with.

I have come to believe that it is almost impossible to love someone who does not love themselves. They always seem to have a way of **not** letting love sink in. It keeps bouncing off them. That is terrible and sets up that person and the person struggling to love them for failure in their relationship. I have experienced this dynamic. It sets up a vicious cycle that I am all too aware of. I want to give you an example of something that just happened the morning I wrote it down. It gave me some very good insight into myself:

I had a very good gentleman friend. I had known him for about three years. He had had a rough background also, so we could relate. I was telling him about my feelings of shame that surface from time to time. He expressed that all he saw was a remarkable woman whom he admired. That was very sweet of him to say, but I blocked it out. I did not let it sink in because it was not consistent with how I felt about myself. However, that was how I needed to see myself from the inside out. It cannot work to keep looking for validation from the outside to try and change the inside, which had been my pattern in the past, but I was not aware of it.

I seemed to gravitate to people like myself who also rejected good feelings from others and were incapable of accepting positive strokes so no real love could develop. I still find those people today, but now I am beginning to see that pattern and what I need to change. Seeing myself bonding with people who could not see the good in themselves was an insightful experience for me. If I was still attracted to this kind of person, it revealed more about me and my struggles with low self-esteem and not liking myself.

Now I see it clearly for what it is. Thank God for one step forward for me on the long road called life. The lesson here is, when I see myself entering into a relationship with a damaged person, to step back and give it some thought. This is a red flag flying high. Don't get me wrong—I am not saying not to have anything to do with wounded people. I can still have a casual friendship and learn many things. But I should not marry someone who is severely damaged and try to fix him as I have done in the past. That is called control and codependency among other things. I have three ex-husbands (Dan, John, and Phil) to prove this does not work. I truly need to feel, know, and see myself as a strong, lovable, remarkable woman. God wants me to know that I am capable of giving and receiving love. Only when I truly know this will God be able to bring the kind of husband into my life that He wants for me.

I need to become the kind of person that I want to attract. I cannot say enough how important a good Godly self-image is. One of the keys to a successful relationship with another is to know yourself well and have a great loving relationship with yourself. Then you can truly give of that love to another. I personally have not experienced this yet, but to have an awareness and understanding of it is the first big hurdle jumped over. I do believe that in the years to come I will enjoy a healthy relationship with a Godly husband. I press on and do the hard work on me. It is not always fun but well worth the effort. Sometimes I get impatient, but God says to "be still, and know that I am God" (Psalm 46:10). His timing is perfect. The verse that comes to mind now is "They that wait upon the Lord shall renew their strength; they shall mount up with wings as eagles; they shall run, and not be weary; and they shall walk and not faint" (Isaiah 40:31).

What a marvelous and refreshing promise from him. I believe that this is what God is asking of me at this point in my life. Another promise is "Seek ye first the kingdom of God, and his righteousness; and all these things shall be added unto you" (Matthew 6:33). How neat is that!

8

Pushing Buttons versus Abuse
How to Tell Them Apart

I have found in writing about abuse and talking about abuse that there are many opinions and misinformation on the subject. I thought I would mention this one dynamic that has come to the forefront for me. I was talking with some friends of mine. When I finished talking about my experience of abuse, one friend said, "Oh, he pushed your buttons."

I was taken aback and surprised. "He pushed your buttons!" To me, this means the person said or did things that they did not know would upset me or make me angry. But after communication the button pushing would stop in a healthy relationship. The incest perpetrated by my father on me was far more damaging than "pushing my buttons." I think I assumed that in this enlightened day and age everyone knows about abuse. Even though there are so many good books written today that explain how to tell if you are abused, so much more education is needed. One might also realize that all the great material in the world will not "educate the masses" if they have no reason to *read* those educational pieces! As I continued to talk with people about abuse, I heard their lack of understanding about what abuse really is. It appears that the major focus is physical abuse, which is much clearer than verbal and emotional abuse. At least everyone seems to be on the same page with the physical form of abuse. Lots of help is available, including the police, shelters, and protection from abuse orders. I do not want to minimize this type of abuse in any way; it is horrible! What I want to explain here is that although "pushing your buttons" can lead to abuse in some cases, it is completely different from abuse. My friend not understanding the difference brought out irritation and frustration in me. I felt misunderstood and a huge lack of connection. I did not share with him how it made me feel. I felt I didn't know him well enough to do that. If I was closer to this person, I would have shared with him what I am telling you. Then the next time I talked with him about abuse, his response would be based on new information that he learned from me. That is a healthy exchange in an abuse-free environment. Learning about abuse and what it constitutes is also a "free will" experience and one not everyone is concerned to learn about. I must accept that as well.

When you discover that something you are doing is bringing out the worst in your friend or spouse, stop it! Do not do it again! Now that seems clear enough and works, except in an abusive relationship. They not only do not stop it; they **do it more often**. The purpose of this is to beat you up with words instead of their fists. This is much more effective over time and not only destroys the relationship but leaves deep emotional wounds that do not heal easily. I know firsthand because this is what Phil did to me, which I will cover more fully later on. I am still working to recover my self-esteem and value. This kind of awareness at a conscious level early in a relationship will save so much pain and heartache later on. I wish I would have known then what I know now. If you are in an abusive relationship, even if it is subtle, they will let you see some red flags if you are educated and paying attention. Listen to your intuition! Women usually have a sixth sense about things and people. We sometimes know something is wrong, but for various reasons, we dismiss it. Do not explain away the behaviors in your head as I did. You can learn from my mistakes. Having self-love, and confidence in one's self-worth, already discussed at length, is key to having the courage to call "foul" on even subtle abuse early on!

Me, age 2.

Me (front), age 4.

Me, age 7, garden duty.

Me, age 9.

Me (left), age 8.

Me, age 7.

Me, age 5.

Me with my parents in 2009.

9

Healing through Writing

I have found great comfort in writing. Included in this chapter will be some of my journal entries, as well as some writing about things I was going through at the time.

This letter was written to me by a friend named Pete. It was important to me as my self-esteem took a nosedive after I separated from my third husband, Phil. I met Pete in July of 2009 and we remain good friends today. This letter, written from a safe male friend, meant a lot to me. I keep it in my heart and read it often, especially when I needed encouragement.

November 17, 2009, 1:19 a.m.

Dear Ruth,
You grace my life. That's what I love about you. You love to listen to God. You are a total blessing to me. You are deserving of God's best and He is drawing us to himself that we both may have his best. I'm honored that He has allowed us to encourage each other. Yes, each day that we have is a gift from the gift giver. My heart is filling with gratefulness and sweet anticipation

as I approach the door that will open onto the path set before me and maybe both of us. Desiring his blessing and being permitted to have each day in his tender mercies. What He has given to us is rare and to be held in his high places that He will always be glorified. I thank my Father for you, and I thank you for the beauty and grace of your heart. You are the wine that He created and was served last. Jesus saved the best for last, a new beginning.

Thanks for being you,
Your Forever Friend 🌻

I had sent Don, my former therapist, a message informing him about my life and the situation with my husband at the time:

Hi Don,
I hope all is well with you and your family.
I know this is not what you wanted to hear, but two months ago I finally left Phil. We had eight months or more of therapy with Emily. Phil remained defensive and blaming. Nothing changed and in fact got worse. He became more abusive as he continued to resent me for making him go to therapy when it was clear he really did not want to go. He never did want to change or do the work. Everyone else wanted it but him. So sad! He told me he was just going to therapy because if he didn't I would leave him. So the bottom line is I just could not do it anymore and keep myself together. I started losing my mental health from the verbal abuse and I had to get out. Emily said she cannot picture Phil ever changing. His walls are too solid and he wants to keep it that way. I am beginning to think I just need to let go as hard as that is for me. I really wanted our marriage to work in the worse way. After we left the south Phil has never had a desire to work through anything to reconnect sexually again. It has been two and half years now and no positive results. I have been so deeply hurt by this and the whole thing I don't think I will ever love him again. He will never change and acknowledge the hurt he has caused me. I will never forget what you told me that love dies of natural causes if not nurtured and taken care of. Many times your insights came back to me and gave me strength when I thought I could not go on. Thank you for the help that at least I received from you. My daughters are sad but very supportive.

Thank you for listening and if you get a chance drop me a line.
Ruth Dormer

His response was timely and expressed gratitude that I had updated him on my life and still cared enough to let people in that I knew cared for me.

Ruth,
It was good to hear from you. I appreciate the update. I'm sorry that your marriage to Phil didn't survive, but I'm not surprised. I was hoping (as you were) that he would step up and drop the defensiveness, but that didn't happen. I commend you for sticking it out and persevering despite the ultimate outcome.
Many blessings on you as you rebuild and seek God's direction for your life. He will restore you.

Blessings,
Don

Here is a journal entry I kept while going through all this. I felt great comfort in keeping a log of what was going on and how I felt. There is more of this diary in Chapter 19.

April 25, 2009

Dear Diary,
I went to a woman's meeting today. It was very encouraging. Here are some thoughts and feelings I took back with me.
Alone we die. With connection we live. We must have a relationship with God and others to live to the fullest, which is God's desire for us all. Our inner critic is the loudest. It is the hardest to forgive ourselves and silence this inner monster. I learned that life is sometimes hard, but God is always good. I want to use my story for God's glory. Then God's glory becomes my story. I love this and want it true in my life. I believe this is His will in all our lives. Blame is an indication of some deep pain. We blame so many things on so many people. Sometimes I feel as though the blame should be directed toward

me. I blamed God, myself, my pastor, and my husband. There are, of course, many others to blame as well. We need healing that only God can provide deep in our soul where the wounding occurred. When we have self-hatred, we begin to die. The great tragedy is what dies inside of us while we live. If we have shame deep inside us, it causes shameful behaviors. Without healing, we look into our past with resentment and blame. We live today angry and we face the future with fear. This is me right now. I feel hopeful after today to be able to accept grace and forgiveness and move on. We cannot control anyone but ourselves. The pain, along with shame and blame, are all a path to nowhere. We do desperate things when we are in pain. The only way to heal is to accept God's grace and forgiveness. Grace is free; all we need to do is receive it. The price has been paid for by Jesus on the cross when He uttered "it is finished." It remains finished. We cannot add or take away anything from that. It is always sad to God when we do not accept the high price He has paid and we attempt on our own to continue to pay. It breaks His heart because He loves us so much! We are His dear children. His desire for us is freedom not bondage. The enemy comes to steal, kill, and destroy. Jesus came that we might have life, and have it more abundantly.

Trauma changed me forever here on this earth. To talk about it helps me make the necessary changes to heal. I must break the silence. When I do, the stronghold is broken. I want to be honest with myself and others. When it is brought out into the light, the darkness flees. That is why Jesus proclaimed that we are the light of the world. He wants us to shine bright for Him. Forgiveness is a long, long journey. The need to punish myself is saying that Jesus did not do enough on the cross. The truth is that our past, our present, and our future sins are totally paid for! What a hard reality for most of us to absorb and practice. Jesus suffered so I do not have to; I can let myself out of prison and be free. God saw me and knew my total life before I was born. He knew what decisions I would make or not make. I am not a surprise to Him. He has a special purpose and plan for you and me. I am an amazing person because of Jesus. God's plan is greater than I could ever think of. I am still a work in progress. We all are. While in pain, my eyes have seen Jesus. I will allow freedom, peace, and joy into my heart. I make a choice to agree with God and release the need to punish myself.

Elmer, who wrote what follows, was Dan's (my ex-husband) best friend.

Mending Your Broken World
By Elmer Kauffman, December 10, 1989

Is your world broken? Are you the victim of an unfair deal?
If you are, then I wonder just exactly how you feel.
Perhaps you've had a problem with your marriage or a friend
or difficulty with your health or bills that never seem to end.
Do the problems that you face often get you down?
Does it seem that even God is nowhere to be found?
Sometimes your heart hurts so much you just don't want to feel,
you wonder if it ever will begin to heal.
If this is you, you have basically three choices to make.
Choose today and don't delay, which one will you take?
Give up and die, do not even try, is choice number one.
It is not my fault, I am not to blame, and no wrong have I done.
Choice number two is like the first, but you decide to live,
but make life rough for everyone and never do forgive.
Choice number three, the best of all, is decide to go on,
and put on the garment of praise whenever things go wrong.
Lift up your head, the word of God tells us to be bold,
for after you have been tried with fire you will come forth as gold.
Put your focus on the Lord instead of on yourself,
for after you have felt the pain you can help someone else.
God will take you through the test; He will not let you fall.
He will work all things out for good if you give him your all.

I could feel the pain and emotion in Elmer's writing. How beyond broken I felt that my marriage of 16 years was over. I wanted to hope with Elmer that my broken world would mend someday. His writing coming from a broken heart helped me see hope that I too will chose to forgive. It encouraged me that I am not alone and each of us would find a path to healing.

10

The Gift of Love and the Burden of Shame

Love is a choice, not a feeling. When we act on that choice, we are usually blessed with warm and loving feelings. Love is easy when returned by the person or whoever our object of love may be. However, it is a whole new concept that Jesus introduced to us. He said to love our enemies and do good to those who despise us. Pray for those that use us. If they ask for our coat, give it to them and bless them. I cannot say that I have experienced this level of love. I am still very much a work in progress. I am forgiven and loved so much by God and others. Yet in my thoughts and heart creep unwanted feelings and choices. I can identify with Paul in the Bible when he says, "What I want to do I don't do. Then when I don't want to do that I end up doing it."

I am glad I am not the only one struggling in this thing called life. How terribly needy we are as people. How valuable grace and forgiveness become in our life as we begin to understand God and His awesome gift of unconditional love for us as His children. How can we not be about our Father's business of sharing the good news that Jesus died for our sins? Why do we let complacency sink in and get so selfish? I asked myself this question many times. Jesus commands us to go into the world and preach the Gospel. Hell is real, and people are dying every day without knowing God. Jesus said we are the light of the world and the salt of the earth. We are to bring the flavor of Jesus' message to all.

God declared that "If my people will humble themselves and pray," He would hear us from heaven and heal our land. We are a very sad nation and in desperate need of healing. When the Enemy comes in like a flood, the Lord will raise up a standard against him. That standard is us. He wants to call His army together for the battle. Christians are God's voice in the land. God's voice needs to be heard when evil rushes in to destroy and silence His voice. Let us all put on the armor of God, pray, and fight the good fight. We are on the winning side, and if God is for us, who can be against us? The Enemy comes to steal, kill, and destroy. He is a liar and the master of lies right from the beginning when he lied to Adam and Eve in the garden. He has been doing it ever since. This is his most effective weapon. Only the light and truth of the Gospel will expose his lies. Let us all humble ourselves, fall on our knees before God, and pray for mercy:

"Lord please open my eyes to really see you. Lead me back home to the safety of your will and eternal life! Amen."

Love people according to knowledge. Love is not judgmental. It is being able to put yourself in someone else's shoes. Maybe if you walked and experienced what they did, you would do worse in life than they did. How do you know? Mercy triumphs over judgment.

James 2:13 says, "Get to know God and His love." Let His love flow through you. Our love has limits. God's love does not. Human love is an incredible thing, the gift that puts purpose in your life and happiness in your heart. God's love is even better. It is the one thing all of us seek in life, whether we realize it or not. If you have found yourself disillusioned with some goal you've chased for years, you are beginning to understand the reason why. That longing you cannot put into words is your soul's desire for God's love. You can deny it, fight it, or try to ignore it, but God's love is the missing piece in the puzzle that is you. You will always be incomplete without it.

Jesus said, "Love one another the way I have loved you." There can be no greater love than this that He lay down His life for His friends. You, my friend, are loved by God more than you can ever imagine. You are special and the apple of His eye.

* * *

Shame came to haunt me once again when I separated from my third husband Phil. I felt like such a terrible failure. The voice of shame whispered to me, "You are unlovable and no one will ever love you." I was struggling also with depression. A few months later, my friend Anne suggested the book *Shame Lifter* by Marilyn Hontz to me. I immediately bought it. What encouragement and strength it gave me to hear the author's challenges also in this area! Reading her book was the beginning of successfully climbing out of the pit called shame.

//
Shame Buster

God's love and forgiveness can pardon and restore any and every kind of sin or wrongdoing. It doesn't matter who you are or what you have done. It does not matter if you have oppressed or murdered. Maybe you have abused yourself or others. The prodigal younger brother in the parable knew that in his father's house there was abundant food to spare. He also discovered that there was grace and forgiveness to spare also. The key was to come home to the Father to receive it. Many times we go away and need to come home again and again. The Father is always the same and comes running out to meet us even before we get there.

Courage is not the absence of fear, but the conquering of it. It is not how many times you fall that matters, but how many times you get up again. Never give up! With God there is always hope and help in time of need.

Shame is a prevailing sense of worthlessness that leads to a false belief that I am what I am and cannot change. I am hopeless. Shame is a feeling that I am defective and the defect is who I am. I am at fault. It is never the victim's fault. There was nothing they could have done to stop the abuse. The shame is not theirs; it belongs to the perpetrators. There are no exceptions to this. Abuse victims develop a shame-based personality and perspective of life. Shame hits you at the core of who you are and says you are a mistake. Guilt says you made a mistake. There is a total difference between shame and guilt. Healthy guilt has an element of hope attached to it. An error has been revealed, yet you are hopeful that a positive change will take place as you address your shortcomings. Shame leaves you feeling helpless; after all, it tells you that something at the very core of your being is defective. Unhealthy, toxic shame is destructive and gives you a sense of worthlessness. The results of toxic shame are serious and long lasting. People affected by it judge themselves as bad, rather than judging their actions as imperfect. They live in terror of unexpected exposure, of others seeing them as they see themselves. This is inner torment as it forbids you to be human, which leads to being isolated and lonely. Once toxic shame is internalized, it runs on autopilot. It can be triggered without anyone doing anything to you. Your own thoughts set it off. This toxic shame expresses itself as inner torment. Continual negative self-talk can be a dead giveaway that toxic shame is present. Shame shuts you down on the inside. The harvest of shame can be bitterness and negative self-talk. Its most beguiling fruit, however, is that of lies, internal lies. They are lies about me, lies from the enemy of my soul. Unlearning the shame language, when we live with shame for an extended period of time, we pick up an additional language. This shame language has a dialect all its own called lies. I am beginning to unlearn the shame and feel loved like crazy by God. You are infinitely loved just as you are. Not as you will be, or could be, or might have been, but just the way you are this minute. To love myself is to accept God's definition of me, not my own.

12

Grief and Forgiveness

After years apart from Dan, living and raising my girls, in May 1998, I got married again. John was charming and passionate, and I fell hard and fast. We got engaged on the third date. Eight months later, we were married. It ended about as fast and furious as it began. Around three months into it, we were fighting and in deep trouble. He had two boys and my youngest daughter was living with us also. It was a blended family that never did blend. I do not think the marriage would have made it regardless.

One undeniable contributing factor to its inevitable end was a tragic phone call. The date was January 12, 1999. I can still feel the trauma to my body this many years later as I think and write about it. The message was kind, but very to the point. Dan (my first husband) had passed away in the hospital. I was in disbelief and shock. It couldn't be! There must be some mistake. He was only 47 years old and healthy. I didn't think it was possible. My precious daughters became my immediate concern. I needed to get to them as fast as possible. How were they going to live without their father? They were so close to him. They really loved him; they still needed him. They were only 21 and 13. Surely this was only a bad dream and soon I would wake up. I was in a panic and did not know what to do. Jennifer was at work as a hairdresser. Angela was in school. I felt compelled to drive to school and tell her that her beloved father was gone. I couldn't allow someone else to give her the news.

Looking back, I don't know how I did it. I was not fit to drive but got there somehow. The school called her out of the classroom. I sat her on my lap and told her that Daddy went to heaven today. Katie, Dan's sister, was there. She drove us to the ER to see him. Angela got sick on the way and threw up. It was the beginning of yet another terrible time in all our lives. Meanwhile, John totally lacked empathy with this loss. He couldn't understand how an ex-husband could generate such turmoil upon his death. John and I were already struggling terribly. Was it jealousy? Who knows? I didn't care at that time. My daughters' welfare was my only concern. I suspect, looking back, that Dan's death hit me personally so hard that I transferred my feelings to concern for my girls. I'm still wrestling with what other unresolved emotions I may have had at that time about my marriage to Dan. I'd been content to blame him for so long, but now, having had great insights to my past and how it affected my marriage to Dan, there were many unresolved issues for me. This threatened my life also! I was consumed with indescribable grief. If I had not had my children to focus on, I believe I would have had a serious mental breakdown.

I took Angie and promptly moved away from John to deal with the grief. She was my first priority. I felt compelled to get her to a safe place for healing. She was devastated and had a long road to recovery. There would be so much pain, depression, withdrawal, and eventually therapy. I'm not sure how one can totally "heal" or recover from such a premature loss of someone so close.

What I believe happened for my daughters and me is that, through the process of time, we formed a new normal. Life goes on, but nothing is ever the same again. Dan will always be missed, whether I speak of him or not. He missed Angie's college graduation. He was greatly missed at my daughter Jennifer's wedding in 2012. I, even as his ex-wife, still struggle with this loss at times today. It remains at the top of my list of the most painful events of my life, to date, as an adult. One of the many reasons I believe it hurts so much is that I wanted my children to have the father I never had. They had that, and then it was painfully and prematurely taken away.

I was angry at God—and at whoever else was handy. Recovery was complicated by the healing I was struggling to do from my own past. Accepting Dan's premature death has been long and hard for the girls and me. I felt so alone with my grief because I was his ex-wife. Nobody seemed to understand why I would still care or have any emotional investment. Of course I know that his loss would affect my girls for the rest of their lives. Our grief would never totally be over!

Dan had been remarried for three years when he passed. After his death, everything fell apart as if hit by rapid fire from a well-loaded machine gun. John was furious that I had left him, and he immediately filed for divorce. Three months later, it was final. I was deep in grief and sorrow such that I barely remember that marriage.

The depth of the grief I felt at Dan's passing may cause you to question what else lay within the emotions that unfurled besides the loss of my girls' father. I never knew such a loving father myself, so I figured it was just that I wanted my daughters to have that and it was taken from them way too early. Dan was a great father and showed it. What a sense of loss there was, on so many levels. Even though Dan is no longer with us on this earth, his contribution lives on. He made more of a difference in his short life than many people ever do. The heart of God is service and sharing the good news of the Gospel. He got this, and I am still learning. I struggle to get past myself. My desires are sometimes too selfish. God is still working on me and taking me to a higher place. Jesus said, "Narrow is the way that leads to life and few people find it." I want to be one of the few who make a difference in this world. I want to hear the words that I am sure Dan heard when he met Jesus: "Well done, good and faithful servant. Enter into your reward" (Matthew 25:23). Today he is enjoying life at the feet of Jesus whom he served and loved.

After Dan's death, an unbelievable chain of events began to unfold that still seems like a soap opera on TV. I remember my girls saying that "at least we have Sara" (Dan's second wife, their stepmother), whom they liked and had become close to in those three years that Sara was married to Dan.

Nobody could have guessed that Sara was about to cause them even more pain. Soon after Dan's death, Sara began dating one of my sister's estranged husbands. Sara and my sister's husband worked together in the same office. My sister and her husband were separated at the time, but not divorced. My sister was seeking to reconcile, but her husband wanted to rush a divorce through so he could legally pursue Sara. My sister gave in and signed the divorce papers.

Eight months after Dan's death, Sara was married again. All of a sudden, while still reeling from losing their father, my daughters' cousins suddenly became their aunt's new stepchildren. Sara, wishing to set up shop and take the bull by the horns, set out to throw herself completely into her new life.

My daughters were left in the dust. They felt abandoned at being dropped by Sara like a hot potato. The machine gun kept on firing, as Sara quickly sold the home that the girls grew up in to move into the home where my sister and her husband had lived. The love and commitment my daughters had enjoyed from their stepmother Sara came crashing down in a million tiny pieces at their feet and would never be put together again. This pain is ongoing and will last a lifetime.

All of these incredible soap opera things happened in the same year (1999) that my sister Darlene committed suicide. Sara and her fiancé were at Darlene's funeral. I remember being very angry because they were there. First, he had pushed through a divorce from my other sister to be with Sara. Second, they were hanging all over each other acting all gooey-eyed, which was totally inappropriate at a funeral and especially in front of the family on whom they had inflicted such a recent divorce. The narrow view of fundamentalist thinking was represented by the pastor who conducted the funeral. He would not let my sister sing at her own sister's funeral because she was divorced. But that same preacher thought there was nothing wrong with her ex-husband serving as a pallbearer. The whole thing was so bizarre that I still have trouble believing that some of these things actually happened.

Most of us were in such shock and grief that no one took it upon them to confront the wrongdoing at that time. The very sad situation of my sister's death was only compounded by another sister's spouse being inappropriate in front of the family and adding to everyone's discomfort and suffering.

People are vulnerable at a time like this and are easily manipulated. With two sudden and unexpected deaths coupled with a hurry-up divorce and then Dan's widow making a play for my sister's husband, it was all very bizarre and surreal.

Thirteen years later, I believed the girls and I had worked hard to forgive Sara. I, however, do not want to see her or have her in my life in any way. I can do that, but my sister cannot. Her children are Sara's step-children, which is a very painful place to be. To be honest, she is handling it better than I would. She really has no choice if there is to be peace in her life. Sara did pay a high price. She was hated by the new stepchildren for the first couple of years because of how fast she did things and how she pushed aside my children and pushed their mother out of the picture. She appeared to have no regard for how her choices would affect others. It was all about her. My sister said to me that Sara has changed and sees the error of her ways. I don't know; I hope this is true. I have not spoken to her in all these years about the terrible pain that she caused. I guess maybe this might still be ahead of me to do, or it may be that this is one area where I can leave that up to God.

It still amazes me that I have to continue to forgive Sara over and over again. When the anger and resentment begin to surface, I need to recommit to God's way and not mine. Another thing that helps me is to remind myself how much I am forgiven. I have hurt people too! They are going through the same process of forgiving me. In Christ's teaching of the Lord's Prayer, it was no mistake that he stated, "Forgive us as we forgive others."

* * *

My daughter Jennifer wrote this tribute in memory of her dad and read it at his funeral. It showed me that Jennifer's faith was strong, and that is what she would rely on to carry her through the grief and loss up ahead.

To Daniel Esh
A Tribute, written by Jennifer Esh on January 15, 1999

Our sorrows will last but for a time. Please Lord put your hand in mine, in heaven to spend days of no end. One's left to mourn, their spirits torn. Sadness extinct, no amount of pain, a body lost, with much to gain. Someday soon I'll see your face, where tears are no longer a trace. God blessed me with one so dear. Forever must my heart be near. A father's love that could only come from above. A gift to me now I give back to thee.

Once you have loved ones in heaven, it changes how you live your life on this earth. I have one piece or two of my heart in heaven while here because my loved ones are already there. It causes me to be homesick at times to see and to be where they are. Yet I would not want to make it happen faster than it is supposed to. I just want my gift of life to make a difference while I am here. I feel more desperate for souls to be saved and have the same hope. Facing hell and eternity without God is one of the most horrible things I can imagine. Lately I have had more of a desire and urgency to spread the good news of Jesus Christ as Savior to whomever I meet. Time is so short and nothing but God's word can be depended on to give us the hope and security that we long for. All else is vanity and loneliness. God put a hole in our hearts that is intended for only Him to fill. I know I struggle to stay connected to that supernatural source. I try to fill the hole with sinking sand, and when I do, that is what I get: a sinkhole.

Jesus said it plainly in the story of building your home on the sand or the solid rock, which is Him, the chief cornerstone. I have a heart for the people in Lancaster city as I drive by them to work every day. I wonder who they are. I see loneliness and fear in their eyes. I want to stop and talk with them. This can only be God wanting to use me, because I have never felt this stirring before in my life. Jesus said that the harvest is plentiful but the labors are few. He told us to pray to him that more workers will be sent out to the harvest field. I find myself praying that way lately. Sometimes it is overwhelming to think of the needs of my neighbors, let alone the whole world. Then when life gets hard for me, I am overcome with how needy I can be and demanding of what I think are my rights. Wow, what would I do without the mighty grace of God that covers all my sin, past, present, and future? He casts them away from me "as far as the east is from the west, so far has He removed our transgressions from us" (Psalm 103:12). How can I not have a tremendous burden for the lost? God's heart has to be broken over the multitude with blinded eyes that cannot and will not see the truth. I want my heart to break for what breaks His. This should always be my prayer every day: "Open up the eyes of my understanding to see You in all the fullness that You desire." Jesus makes it clear when He says that if we only have hope in this life we will be miserable. I guess that explains in part why sometimes I am sour about life. In some ways, in light of eternity, that is normal not to feel totally at home on this earth. It is a very temporary place and not meant to feel like home entirely. The purpose for us to be here on earth is one reason only: to tell the world this message of salvation and preparing ourselves to live forever either in heaven or hell. The choice is ours. God is not willing that any should perish. Hell was created for the devil and his angels when he was thrown out of heaven. But if I insist or you insist on going there, God gave us the choice of free will. However by accepting Jesus' death on the cross, eternal bliss is a blessed reality and joy for you. Why would I not make it my mission in life to take as many precious souls with me to heaven as possible by shouting the warning all over town? The enemy wants to keep me all tangled up in details of this life that mean nothing. If he can have me tired, distracted, and depressed, I will stay blinded to God inching me forward with a greater vision than my own. As one of my good friends put it, the hardest thing sometimes is to be still, patient, listening for his direction. When our path is ordered by the Lord, success is a guarantee. We must be about our Father's business. Broad is the way that leads to destruction; narrow is the way that leads to life, and few of us find it.

13

Feelings
Loneliness, Love, and Loss

There have always been people that I could be with or be around. There are even wonderful friends in my life. I have had a girlfriend named Anne for over 30 years. She has been with me through thick and thin, though sometimes it seems like mostly thin. Her life has been far from easy also but for some very different reasons. We understand and can relate to each other's struggles. One recurring theme in our lives that we share is depression. One thing sets us apart, and that is that she has been married for over 30 years. That is a story all its own. I have followed the pain and fear in that relationship. It sure is not a "happily ever after" story. Nevertheless, she has three children and three beautiful grandchildren. I feel like she has made the right decision to stay married, accept him, and make the most of it. A part of me is envious. I don't know why, except that I still have a belief that married people do not feel lonely. In my head, I know that is not true and an unrealistic expectation of marriage, but I want to cling to it anyway.

After all, it is still a couples' world. It has to be easier in many ways when there are two instead of one. I know there are many verses in the Bible to support this. God said that it is not good for mankind to be alone.

I am sure this is not just referring to the obvious one, meaning marriage. I think of the flood and how He sent the animals into the ark two by two. I am single after three failed marriages. Today I feel lonely. I know I could talk to Anne and she would understand. But I don't call her or make any attempt to get together. Sometimes I feel like avoiding her, perhaps because of envy that her marriage has stayed together.

I have asked myself many questions lately. What is really going on? Am I going into some kind of cave? Is this a good thing or bad? How do I know?

The only thing that is consistent is the ache of loneliness. I know marriage will not fix it, but what will? I am searching to get in touch with deeper feelings under the surface. What I do have is a vague feeling that there is a little girl inside me that still cries for her daddy. Perhaps that is still the root of it all. Maybe it is like what people call a "new normal" after a loss. You never really totally recover. Learning to live and cope with loneliness never going away no matter what I do is a new concept. I keep looking for a cure, and maybe there is none. What if the answer would lie in acceptance? I am not alone by any means. This is probably one of the many feelings that people try to drown out by drugs, alcohol, sex, food, excessive work, or anything to go unconscious, if even for a short time, to get relief from the emotional pain.

One friend of mine seems to think that feelings are the enemy. The answer, according to her, is just not to feel. I've already attested to the fact that in my post–abuse period, I coped by not feeling and it cost me dearly! But feelings have a way of clobbering us over the head for attention. We have all kinds of defenses against painful feelings. The sad thing about this is that the *good feelings are blocked out as well*. Anesthetized to feelings, we can appear to be stable and strong, but we are living the life of a robot. For anyone like me who grew up with a rule against feeling, it's a lifetime struggle to legitimize the feelings. Some decide, maybe not even on a conscious level, never to take the chance of being vulnerable and open to hurt again.

At the age of 61, I am discovering it is more and more difficult to take risks, but without risks my life would be stymied. Sometimes, I become aware of my feelings when I have already acted on them, which is usually not a good thing. Then I have to backtrack and try to figure out, what was I thinking? And what was I feeling when I did that? I know that I will continue the search for a healthy emotional life and relationship. It may always be a hard road, but I am stubborn and will not ever give up. I am looking for love, but what kind? I am aware of God's great unconditional love. Shouldn't that be enough?

Some Christians say so to me, and that if it isn't, there is something wrong with me. I think some of what I long for is a human being to love me in a way that *demonstrates* the way God loves. I desire a love that will draw me closer to Jesus and cause me to grow in my understanding of Him. I want an example like what Jesus showed people love was. I realize people all are only human like me. Even if I find a man who truly loves me, he will make mistakes and I will get hurt. I want to learn what a healthy relationship is rather than a perfect one, which does not exist. I am finding it takes a lot of effort to be honest with myself and others when it involves feelings. I believe it may be wise to take the time to get a refresher course in therapy after this third divorce. At the time I first wrote this, it had been two years and I was struggling to find a place of peace and direction for my life. I am in touch with the fact that if I allow myself to be around an emotionally unavailable person, it makes it almost impossible to be in touch with my feelings. Now I know what not to do. I am still in the process of identifying those who are not healthy for me and staying out of an intimate relationship with them. My loneliness increases when I am with that kind of person. I need to run away and see that I am better alone than with someone who has a wall of defenses that will not come down around his feelings. I have discovered that sometimes Christians are worse with feelings than nonbelievers. This should not be so and is very sad to me. I think if they really knew Jesus, they would know He was a very emotionally healthy person with strong feelings, including passion and anger.

14

Grief and Letting Go
(September 25, 2012)

My mother is 91 years old. She lies comfortable in her bed. She is still alive, but I am beginning to grieve as if she were dead. I know she loves the Lord with all of her heart. What a great treasure awaits her when she departs. For six long months now, I have missed her voice and beautiful smile. Even though I am sad, it makes me glad to know that we will be reunited in just a little while. I kiss her, tell her that I love her, and will always be near. I believe she can hear me; sometimes I think I see the hint of a tear. She wished me a happy birthday, which is the last time I heard her speak. It was when I turned 61, a beautiful memory I will always keep. I don't know how long yet until we have to say goodbye, but the time will be short and the next word from her will be "Hi!"

She believed in the wonderful promise of eternal life. With much love and prayer, she passed it on to me. I am certain my mother will hear words of comfort, as she worships at the feet of Jesus, God's precious Son.

So as I grieve and let go of her here on this earth,
I look forward to that new body and birth.

83

It is only the beginning of a brand-new life.
No more tears, pain, sorrow, or strife.
What a joyful time in eternity we will share,
never more a worry or care.
No more parting from loved ones in heaven it will be;
Jesus said to comfort each other with these words until His face we see.

* * *

My mother gave me the following poem when I was in grief about six months after Dan died. My mother read and wrote poetry. I saved it because it came from her. I came across it again while writing this book and wanted to include it as it is a reminder of how God takes care of me and holds me in His hands.

The Rose
Author Unknown

It's only a tiny rosebud,
a flower of God's design,
but I cannot unfold the petals
with these clumsy hands of mine.
If I cannot unfold a rosebud,
this flower of God's design,
then how can I think I have the wisdom
to unfold this life of mine?
So I'll trust Him for His leading
every moment of every day.
And I'll look to Him for his guidance
each step of the pilgrims' way.
For the pathway that lies before me
my heavenly Father knows.

I'll trust Him to unfold the moments

just as He unfolds the rose.

Authorship for this poem has been claimed in several different names, including Era Earlene Fleming; Charlie Gilchrist; Vernie McMqueen [*sic*] White; Rev. Vaughn Morton of Fresno, California; and I. H. Terry of Bakersfield, California. However, the most insistent claim of authorship comes from Rev. Darryl L. Brown of Lithia Springs, Georgia. It is shown here as my mother wrote it out.

15

Friendship Evangelism
Reaching Out to the Lord

I have been asking myself some questions lately about sharing the good news of the Gospel with people. What is the best way to approach people? Each person is different, so how do you share with them in a way that really will make them want what I have? I have heard and seen many different teachings and theories. There are some ways of sharing the good news that makes it actually sound more like bad news. It causes people to want to run away from us. If this happens, how can we still make an impact? This is the last thing that I would want as the result. I have recently become more aware of learning how Jesus did it. He was like a magnet and people were drawn to Him. They strained to hear what He was saying when He spoke to the multitudes on the hillside. What was it about Him that I need to study, read, and learn about? I do know that some ways are more effective than others. I believe in *friendship evangelism* even though it takes a lot of time and patience to build a relationship with someone. It appears to me that most Christians stick to their own kind and do not venture too far out of the fold. Also the need for study on wisdom and discernment from the Holy Spirit is a given. The religious people of Jesus' day got the worst words from the Master. They hated Him but sinners loved him. I believe sinners felt the love and compassion He had for them. He gently led them into the fold.

He met them right where they were and spoke in terms they understood. He gave them no judgment. Jesus said, "I have not come to call the righteous but sinners" to repentance. Those who were sure they were righteous people were threatened by Him. They had religion but did not know Jesus' heart through a personal relationship. I often hear someone say "I am not very religious" when I attempt to share the good news. I usually reply back to them that I am not at all religious. That gets their attention and maybe a chance to talk about a personal relationship based on Jesus' work on the cross. Man looks on the outward appearance and Jesus sees the heart. Law and religion alone kill, but the Spirit gives life. My heart is burdened for the lost. I am going to pray and ask God for divine appointments with those he has prepared. I do not want opportunities to be squandered. No meeting or relationship is by chance. God brings those into our sphere of influence for a reason. I hope that the ones I touch have been brought closer to God because of knowing me, if for only a short time or one encounter. Our steps are ordered by the Lord and we need to follow His lead. To hear His still, small voice in this loud busy world is a big challenge and takes a conscious effort on our part. I sometimes confess that I am lazy and complacent. I know the lies from the Enemy to me that say I am not good enough. Jesus said that Satan is the accuser of the brethren, not Him. In the letter to the Romans, St. Paul declared that there is no condemnation of those who walk not after the flesh but after the Spirit. When the woman caught in adultery was brought before Him, Jesus said, "Let him who is without sin cast the first stone." They all hung their heads and walked away.

Jesus said, "Neither do I condemn you; go and sin no more."

She ran into the village to tell everyone what he did for her.

Wow, wouldn't that be wonderful if we had that response from someone! I can picture myself praying for someone to be healed and she is mightily touched by God. In my mind's eye, she is running to all her friends to tell them the good news of salvation and healing, just like the woman at the well. I believe that I will live to see that day. God wants to anoint my hands with His healing power for spiritual, physical, and emotional healing. I myself need to learn to receive more from what He wants me to have so I can share with and help others. It has been a very long and difficult road to get past my own issues to even begin thinking of others. I want to do more than just survive. My goal is to thrive and grow strong and healthy in the Lord. Of course, this is easy to say but much harder to do. I am not alone, though, and cannot do it with just my own strength. As St. Paul said, "When I am weak, then I am strong," because I need to depend on my Lord. Let us go forth with daring and courageous living, chasing our dream that was put inside us. Let us be vulnerable and worthy of giving and receiving love. It will transform the way we live and lead others. How very imperative it is that we feel lovable on the inside or we will not allow anyone to love us. I will only let in what I feel like I deserve.

No matter how much someone loves me, if I feel unlovable, their love will be repelled and just run off my heart like rain off a duck's back. As hard as it is sometimes, the truth of the matter is that love works from the inside out. Only then will you be able to experience true love. Just today I told my friend that I love her, and her reply was a one-word answer: "Why?" I do not know for sure what was behind that, but I suspect that she has low self-esteem and does not feel lovable or worthy of love on the inside, so she has no idea why anyone would love her or even want to for that matter. I myself can identify with this struggle. The saying "It takes one to know one" is true. I have been through three marriages and three divorces, and I am well aware that I am capable of sabotaging love or repelling it. I know the search for love will be futile until I do the inside work in my heart. I need to see myself as lovable and worthy of being fully loved simply because God says so. I receive His truth, and it becomes real in my heart and feelings. What comes natural to me, sometimes on an unconscious level, is my avoidance of vulnerability. Some of this is necessary and healthy to keep harmful people out. It is just as important to learn when it is safe to open up and let someone love me. I am very good at keeping everyone at a safe distance and I always have an exit strategy. I am terribly aware of my fear in this area. I can run away before I even realize that I am running. The great news for me—and you—is that when stuff comes to a conscious level, healing and growth is only one more step away.

Inspiration, March 19, 2000
Written by Robert Walker, one of my dear friends!

He walks with me and talks with me while the dew is still on the roses. How wonderful it is that He walks with us and talks to us. And to have those roses and to have them sparkle with dew, there had to be rain and storms. That, along with the sun, is what makes things grow. But the real wonder is that He is there also when the storms rage and the winds howl and the claps of thunder attempt to destroy our faith and joy. He is there when it is a moonless night and the roses in the garden make us afraid. He is there in the garden all the time ready to walk with us and talk to us all the time. How often we fail to reach out in the storms waiting for daybreak. How wonderful to reach out when life and yes we are at the worst point, and touch Him. At all times He is there. At all times reach out to Him.

16

Songs

I wrote these songs out of pain and struggle. I would cry out to God and then write. They encouraged me because I felt the words were from God. I felt His presence and knew I was not alone. My songs were therapeutic for me, and I hope they will be for others as well.

1973

1. He Will Answer
If you will go with Jesus, then He will go with you.
If your feet do stumble, He will also be with you.
You will find He loves you
more than what you've ever known.
Just fall to your knees in prayer,
and Jesus will meet you there.
I heard him whisper to me,
"My child, some day you will see,
just trust me one more day,
and I will roll the clouds away.

If you keep your eyes on Me,

then the sunlight you will see."

When the tears start to fall,

on His Name you will call.

After I have talked with Jesus, and He has talked with me,

I get up off my knees, and I see things differently.

Chorus:

He will answer; He will answer, with a message loud and clear:

"I love you, I love you, and I am always near."

2. Trains

Why is it that when I see trains go by

deep within me something begins to stir?

There's a gentle tug at my heart, and I sigh,

as I push the feeling down again and wonder why.

The days go by and I'm busy when all of a sudden I hear it again.

The distant sound of a whistle blow,

my heart beats faster within me,

and then once more I am filled with woe.

Time goes on and still I feel

that something within me just will not heal.

That part of me that longs to be

on a train that comes by me.

It has been a long time now and I thought it was gone,

but in the next hour it proved me wrong.

I saw a train go by so slow,

then my heart very much wanted to go,

but once again I sadly said no.

1974

1. Nothing's Impossible

My God knows what's best for me. He tells me in His word to trust.

My future is in His hands. So I think it best just to rest.

He speaks in that still small voice, saying "Nothing's impossible for Me.
You don't understand how it could be,
but I am working out what is best for thee.
The time will come when the path is clear, and you can see what lies ahead.
But as for now, I am still near,
just trust me and be of good cheer.
I will guide you through the rocks and stones.
When there seems to be no way,
look up and pray,
for can't you see that nothing is impossible for Me.
'Some things are just too hard for God' I seem to hear you say,
but I will lead you day by day.
I will show my plan for you until at last you see
that I am God and nothing is impossible for me."

2. God's Promises

God promised to stay every day;
He brings me back when I stray.
Oh sinner can't you hear
Him whisper in your ear:
"My love is reaching down for you."
He promised to save you today;
if you ask Him, He will show you the way.
But if you turn down the Savior's call,
His promises are not for you at all.
You are weary, and the way seems long.
But there is hope for you in this song.
Listen to Jesus say, "Come and rest."·
This is the promise that I like best.
Chorus:
God promised to love me and guide me;
He's always beside me.
His promises are sure, His promises are true,
and He's coming back for you.

3. Jesus on Your Mind

There's a message I am bringing to you,
my friend; it's telling me what to do.
The storm will come, and the thunder will roll.
Darkness will sweep over my soul.
But here is the secret I want you to know:
just think of Jesus, and the burden has to go.
Your mind is filled with worry and care,
about what the future may hold.
Each day gets longer, the rest shorter,
until suddenly you feel awfully old.
So now I know it is time you are told:
Jesus never intended for you to carry that load.
It is time to stop, look, and listen to what the Master has to say.
The answer lies in His spoken Word. With Jesus there is always a way.
If only you turn your mind on Him, and to your Savior pray.
Chorus:
Oh what a happy time with Jesus on your mind.
Oh what a happy time with Jesus on your mind.
Jesus in the morning, Jesus in the noontime,
What a happy time with Jesus on your mind.

4. One Lonely Night

I came to God one lonely night, at the end of a long hard day.
I felt I used up all my strength; I am even too tired to pray.
I knew I had asked God many a time
about this same problem of mine.
I began to wonder if I wearied God if I asked Him once again.
As I fell to my knees and began to pray,
God seemed a million miles away.
I cried, "O God, are You still there?"
My burden seemed more than I could bear.
I said, "God, do You really care?

Are You listening to what I say?"

Then He began to answer me, with a voice loud and clear.

Suddenly I knew my Lord was very near.

Then to me I heard Him say,

"You may come to Me any day.

Tell me what troubles you; I am always ready to hear. You may not understand,

but dare to trust Me, and you will see,

I knew all along how your life would be."

I felt His loving arms wrap themselves around my heart,

and then I knew for certain that my God and I would never part.

1975

1. God

If I know my heart today, I don't desire wealth or earthly fame.

My desire isn't to make for myself a name.

God, You know my heart today, I want to show some soul great love,

and how Jesus came down from above.

He died on the cross for man's sins and mine;

He paid the price for all time.

God, help me not to look at what others do,

but to get my guidance and direction from You.

Sometimes I forget that You are leading me, Lord,

and I follow someone I greatly admire,

but they don't know of my deepest desire,

which burns inside me like unquenchable fire.

I pray, dear God, that You will set me free,

from worrying about what others think of me,

to live, to sing, to serve, to pray,

in my own special way.

God, You see deep down inside,

and I know that You are satisfied.

So help me, God, to be today

what I know You want me to be,

so that You can live Your life through me.

2. Peace

When God tests me, it tries my faith.
Sometimes I wonder and hesitate.
Then I am called to that hour of prayer.
God said, "I will meet you there."
God gave peace to my troubled heart.
More of His love He did impart.
When fear of the future crowded my mind,
God said, "I am the master of time."
High on the mountain things look bright.
Now I see God was right.
I am glad that I was fed in the valley below.
God said, "Now you have strength to go."
Now I have learned to trust Him more.
Now we are closer than ever before.
His word is hid deeper down in my heart.
God said, "I will never depart."
Chorus:
Yes, I'm in the valley; I don't know why.
Jesus loves me, so I wouldn't cry.
I will lift my face to heaven and praise His Holy name,
for Jesus is with me just the same.

3. Calvary

How well do I remember the darkness of that night?
God had spoken to my heart, and I knew He was right.
He asked me to open up and let Him come in.
He promised light for darkness and freedom from sin.
Since I opened up my heart, Jesus has come in.
He has always kept his word, He took away my sin,
now I am walking by His side,
and He's a constant friend and guide.
He promised light for darkness and freedom from sin.
As I journey down life's road, troubles come my way,
but joy and peace can still be mine,

because Jesus said He would stay.

Through it all, I am glad to say

Jesus rolled the clouds away.

He promised light for darkness and freedom from sin.

Chorus:

Oh, yes I've been to Calvary, I can say I've seen the light.

Oh yes I've been to Calvary, and I can say I've been redeemed.

Oh come, my friends, to Calvary,

He'll do the same He did for me.

Oh come today,

and don't delay

to Calvary.

4. Strength

When I was in doubt, I turned to God

with questions in my heart.

I felt like He didn't know I walked this sod.

I thought for sure He did depart.

Then I heard His voice again.

Once again my Lord came through

when I did what He told me to.

The sun shone bright and the things we shared,

I knew He really cared.

He assured me one more time

that there is strength for every trial.

Chorus:

Yes, there's strength for every trial,

and there's grace for every mile.

I found it so just now.

I found it so just now.

1976

1. Out of Touch

As I walk along down life's pathway,

sometimes I lose my way.

But then I hear my Savior say,
I am only a prayer away.
The sky grows dark, and the thunder rolls,
and the lightning will never stop.
But Jesus says, "Just call on Me;
I will always see you through."
Out of touch with Jesus,
that's when I stumble and fall.
He picks me up and says,
"Next time, remember to call."
Troubles come and I don't understand
just why some things must be.
But this one thing I learned for sure:
It's all right if I talk with the Lord.
Chorus:
Jesus is all I need.
Jesus is all I need,
with His hand in mine
till the end of time.
My Jesus is all that I need.

1979

1. Loving Me

I wandered down that lonesome highway,
away from God and what He had for me.
Then I heard, heard my name in love:
"Come home, My child. I'm love. I love you."
Coming back to my loving Father,
we share the joy we lost along the way.
Then I know, oh yes I know.
I'm coming home. He's love. He loves me.
It doesn't matter where I go,
His love will follow me; this I know.
I can trust his hand of mercy
to guide me through with love; He loves me.

Chorus:

Loving me, oh yes, loving me.

He loves me back into the fold.

1980

1. Day Star

Jesus is the Light that shines in a dark place.

By walking in the Light, I know I am always safe.

Wherever the Light goes, darkness has to flee.

I know that darkness will never get a hold on me.

That Light is like the beauty of the day dawning,

giving way to the sun of hope, new life spawning.

Growing and reaching those new heights to climb.

There is never an end to where this Light will shine.

Faith will be as the day star arising in your heart,

knowing that you and the Light will never part.

It is steadfast and shining all along life's way.

Giving courage and promise to each new day.

Chorus:

So let the Light shine in a dark place,

smile as the day dawns,

and let the day star arise in your heart.

1981

1. The Word Will Do What It Says

Martha sat at Jesus' feet and cried,

"Master had you been here, my brother wouldn't have died."

Jesus spoke: "Just believe and be free,

because the glory of My God you shall see."

Once you have been freed and forgiven from sin,

don't let that doubt and confusion set in.

You are delivered from the things of yesterday,

so live, act, and talk that way.

There is no fear in perfect love,

coming down from the Father above.
Jesus' love will go on unending,
saving, keeping, and setting hearts free.
Chorus:
The Word will do what It says.
It will not return void.
If you trust It, believe It, and confess It,
the Word will do what It says.

2. God Is Faithful

Peter was walking on the water, with high waves around him, you see.
But eyes of faith don't see them, just Jesus with His outstretched arms.
Peter was fishing on the lake one day
and all night with nothing to show.
By faith they cast on the other side,
with a catch too heavy to tow.
Martha was troubled about many things; the cares of life dragged her down.
When Jesus said, "Come rest awhile," to her ears was a joyful sound.
Whatever your hand finds to do, do it with all your might,
because God says to walk by faith and not to walk by sight.
Chorus:
God is faithful in all things, not willing that any should die.
His mercy and love go on forever. Come to Jesus today and live.

2010

1. Done

How hard it is to trust the One
who has said, "The work is done.
You are forgiven; you can let it go,
for from Me the blood has flowed."
Undeserving am I;
that is why my Savior died.
I no longer have to try;
"It is finished," He did cry.
Let the healing river flow,

because under the Blood it will go.
His love has taken the whole load,
setting me free from the seeds I've sowed.
Trust totally in Jesus as God's Son,
for truly the work He has done.
Guilt and shame must go away,
according to His Word, He has spoken today.
Bridge:
Undeserving am I;
that is why my Savior died.
I no longer have to try;
"It is finished," He did cry.

2012

1. Hold On

"Hold onto Me, my child, don't ever let go,
there is a battle to be fought; trust Me, I know.
I will lead you through the pain and strife;
I am the only one who will get it right.
I know you better than you know yourself;
my love for you is eternal, not like anyone else.
I will give you my peace in place of fear;
that is why to Me you must stay near.
Hold onto Me; that is the only way to see
the miracles unfold in your life; just let it be.
Don't try to run away and hide;
I am the Good Shepherd and guide.
I know sometimes you think the pace is too slow,
but without hearing My Voice it is not safe to go.
Just listen to me whisper; be patient and wait.
When the time is right, I will show you the steps to take."
When I go astray,
and can't find my way,
I know it is time to hear what God has to say.
So easy it is for my heart to sin;

more intolerable still is to justify it within.
I want to be free,
and I know that with God's forgiveness, I will be.
I may not be rich, or have worldwide fame;
I may be no one as far as my name.
I may not sing as well as you;
I may not have eyes that sparkle blue.
I may not be dressed in the latest style,
but that does not make my life worthwhile.
I may think I am too short, or I might be too tall,
but this isn't really what matters at all.
I may not like the look on my face;
to me it is an awful disgrace.
I may be disgusted when I look at my hair,
and it never seems to stay after I have combed it there.
I may not be perfect, as you can see,
but here is the thing that's important to me:
It is about my Jesus Who hung on the tree;
this I am sure wasn't pretty to see.
He bore the sin of the whole human race,
yet I can see love upon His Face.
The most beautiful person that you'll ever see
is the person who loves Jesus as much as me.

17
Starting Over

Before I left Dan in 1991, I knew it would be hard for me without an education to find a good job. Entering the work force after all these years was frightening and intimidating. I had stayed home for my entire first marriage. At my therapist's suggestion, I went to night school for five months to study and get my GED, or high school equivalency degree, from the state. The test was a grueling 16 hours over two days. Looking back I do not know how I did it. I was told when I got the score that I not only passed but I had one of the highest scores they had seen in a long time. I was totally floored. They suggested that I go to college. This was the first time I had ever heard or vaguely considered that I might be smart.

Naturally, with such low self-esteem, I quickly dismissed the college idea. God was faithful to me right where I was. I found a part-time job in a music box store. It was an education to be working again. It was also a lot of fun. Every item in the store played some kind of music. My boss was a Christian and helped me along with encouraging words. My confidence grew. I realized that I *was intelligent* and I learned quickly. I also went back to being a waitress. This was good money because of tips. This arrangement worked for several years, and then in 1994, someone encouraged me again to consider more schooling. I heard lots of talk directed my way about "wasted potential."

Of course, all of this was new to me, but I listened. I began to dwell on the fact that maybe they were right and that I was missing something. This gave birth to an idea to build on my office experience with Elite Genetics. I had done the bookkeeping with Dan for many years. I saw how a business worked. So, with fear, trembling, and much encouragement from my friends, I decided to quit my jobs and go to school. I presented my GED paperwork to Consolidated School of Business and was immediately accepted into the program. I decided to take Computerized General Office Management. I laugh to myself now as I type this because I had no idea what I was getting into. It was a good plan, but there were some things I overlooked. The main thing was that although my GED scores were high, I had never touched a typewriter or a computer. Several days into the program, I found myself in a classroom of high school graduates typing away beside me faster than I could think. I was blindfolded with a special shield so I could not look down and see the keys, only up at the book in front of me, to learn to type. This is when I had my first of many panic attacks. What in the world are they talking about? How do you learn to type without looking where the keys are? This is how little I knew. I had a similar experience looking at a computer screen for the first time. I was frightened out of my mind!

The program was 18 months long. After three days, I really wanted to run away. I felt this whole thing was a big mistake. Had it not been for my instructors, who saw my dilemma and reached out to me, I would have quit. They believed in me and told me they felt that I could learn to type and also learn basic computer skills. I worked hard to tune out all the fast typing around me and focus on my slow pecking. It was really amazing to me how my fingers eventually knew where to go on the keyboard. I had to type 30 words a minute accurately to pass the class. In three months' time, I did just that! I also mastered basic computer skills. I was very surprised at what I accomplished. It seemed no one else was surprised but little ol' no-self-esteem me. The teachers were matter-of-fact that there was never any doubt with them that I could do it. I was only four months into the program when, one day, I was telling my chiropractor, Charles, about my accomplishments at school, and he offered me a front desk job at his practice. Now I had a tough decision! Do I take the job or finish school?

I decided to take the job. I was anxious to get to work. I needed the money and had not been working while in school full-time. I was with Charles for around a year and a half. I learned so much and thoroughly enjoyed the people and my job. It was enough to launch my office career. I went on to get my best job in 1996 at a nonprofit in Lancaster, Pennsylvania. I started out at $10 an hour, which was a huge amount for me. At the interview, I tried to not look surprised when he mentioned the starting salary. I had never made that much in my life and never imagined that I would. I was hired as payroll/benefits administrator.

Once again I had no clue what the job was all about. I had never done anything close to payroll. I was responsible for more than 350 employees' biweekly payroll. The first day on the job, I totally freaked out on the inside. I kept it to myself because I really needed this job and did not want to fail. There was a three-month probation period, which is common with most jobs. I was so overwhelmed with the payroll software and how it worked. I went home many nights and cried myself to sleep. I fully expected to get fired after the 90 days were up.

Somehow again by God's grace and mercy I made it. I got a great review at the end of my probation period and—another miracle to me at that time—a 50-cent-an-hour raise. I cried again, but this time for a different reason. I was beginning to understand how much God loved me and wanted to provide for my needs. He was continuing the good work of healing in me that he had begun and would continue until the end of my life on this earth. I went on to have eight years with this company and many raises. I bought my own home, and by 2004 I was in a good place financially. I thought I had it made. The rest of my life was going to be great. Little did I know that I would soon make a decision that would not only cause me to give up my job, but once again, I would be fighting for my life.

* * *

I can identify with the poem that follows, as I have had to start over many times. I wanted to include it here in my book to encourage you. As long as you are alive and breathing, you can start over. God never gives up on us even when we give up on ourselves.

Start Over
By Woodrow Kroll

When you've trusted God and walked His way,

when you've felt His hand lead you day by day,

but your steps now take you another way—

Start over.

When you've made your plans and they've gone awry,

when you've tried your best and there's no more try.

When you've failed yourself and you don't know why—

Start over.

When you've told your friends what you plan to do,

when you've trusted them and they didn't come through,

and now you're all alone and it's up to you—

Start over.

When you've failed your kids and they're grown and gone,

when you've done your best but it's turned out wrong,

and now your grandchildren come along—

Start over.

When you've prayed to God so you'll know His will,

when you've prayed and prayed and you don't know still—

when you want to stop because you've had your fill—

Start over.

When you think you're finished and want to quit,

when you've bottomed out in life's deepest pit,

when you've tried and tried to get out of it—

Start over.

When the year has been long and successes few,

when December comes and you're feeling blue,

God gives a January just for you—

Start over.

Starting over means "Victories Won."

Starting over means "A Race Well Run."

Starting over means "God's Will Be Done."

Don't just sit there—

Start over!

18

Round Three

It was December 18, 2004. Today was my wedding day to my third husband. I was very nervous, but hopeful that this one would "go the distance." I was really hoping for it to be the marriage I would keep for the rest of my life. I was also looking forward to experiencing real love for the first time. I was 54 years old. Before I go any further, I want to give you a little background about the relationship that led to this third marriage.

I met Phil at a singles volleyball game in 1995. We dated for two years. He lived in Harrisburg and I lived in Lancaster—towns about 35 miles apart. At the end of the two years, we talked about marriage. I had just gotten my good payroll job in Lancaster and did not want to give it up to move closer to him. He had a great job at a steel plant as a crane operator and did not want to quit his job either. We talked about splitting the distance and living halfway between our jobs. Also, at that time my girls' father, Dan, was still very much alive and very involved in the girls' lives, and he did not want me taking them farther away from him. He felt like the distance would cause problems for him. He was concerned that he would not see them as often as he wanted to. For the next six months, Phil and I talked and tried to work things out. In the end, the issues seemed too big to resolve, so around 1997, we broke up.

It was very sad, because my relationship with Phil had been very loving. It was the best one I had ever experienced. We prayed together often and played like kids. We enjoyed tennis, hiking, and talking and called each other *soul mates*. It really was the closest I have ever been to knowing what the term *soul mates* actually meant. I really did not recognize how special and rare this type of relationship was before that experience.

With the benefit of hindsight now, I wish I would have found a way to work it out and not break up with him. I was impatient, and the mountain looked too steep to conquer. The outcome still might have been the same. I had no way of knowing who the real Phil was. I cannot reconcile in my mind the two very different relationships that I had with him separated by only a few years, but things happen to people to change them, and change is a constant.

I worked hard in the years that followed to forgive myself. I made what I thought was the best decision for me and the girls. I moved on, but I could never forget the special relationship he and I had shared.

In 1998, I married husband number two. I told you earlier about that marriage and the tragic death of my daughters' father in 1999. This marriage ended about the turn of the millennium in 2000.

Around this time, I got a call from Phil to express his condolences on my loss of the girls' father. I thanked him and we promised to stay in touch. We spoke on the phone maybe every couple of months or so. It was very causal.

As mentioned earlier, with my raises in my payroll position in 2002, I bought my own home. I called Phil to come and help me move. He came and afterwards, Phil and I and the other movers went out for pizza. It was so good to see him again. For the first time since we split, the thought of getting back together flashed through my mind. We had been apart for five years.

He was still single and had had some relationships in those five years that were not so good and did not work out. The spark was still there between us. He said, however, that he did not want to date again but could use a good friend. So we met for the next six months as friends and got reacquainted with each other. At this point I was falling in love with him again. Phil, however, just wanted to remain friends.

Once again we had a problem. Of course, I took matters into my own hands. I used my feminine powers to convince him that circumstances had changed in our favor and now we could be together. The girl's father had died, so him being near them was no longer an issue as it had been before. By 2004, I was tired of my job and was willing to move to be closer to his work. I did not see any reason why it would not work out this time around. I was missing a key ingredient, however. In my desire to be "connected" and be in a marriage, I failed to see that while I was ready, he was being pushed along against his will. Unfortunately I would not find this out until years later. This turned out to be the first step of many in the wrong direction. I gave him an ultimatum: I wanted all or nothing. If he did not want to date again, I wanted no part of just a friendship. He was lonely and did not want to lose me as a friend, so he agreed to date again. We dated for another two years.

Hindsight is always 20/20 vision, as they say. It seems so clear now. What was I thinking? Everything was different. He was not the same person I had known five years earlier. Our relationship was stressful. No more soul mates. At the time I did not understand where the stress came from. I was very happy to be back with him. All I could see were the memories of how wonderful our time *had been* together those five years earlier.

There were many signs that all was not well with him, but I denied them, as I hung onto the memories of our earlier times. I saw him through the experience of the past. Surely the person I had known was still in there somewhere. I did see a few glimpses of the Phil I had known. Most of our relationship, however, was based on my perceptions of how he had been *before* and denial of the present. I think it was just too painful for me to accept that he had changed. The soul mate connection was gone. I refused to believe that it was gone for good. I made it my mission to encourage him and love harder. I teased him, flirted with him, and pushed him toward marriage. I knew the real Phil was in there—somewhere just waiting for marriage to bring him out of this new "shell" that seemed to envelop him.

Finally, he proposed and I was high as a kite. I got my man and the love of my life. I barely noticed that he had no ring. I just as conveniently dismissed the sad look on his face as I accepted his proposal.

Yes, denial had been my friend and served me well in childhood in order to survive my abuse. I was not aware at the time that *denial* would now be my downfall, and not my salvation. Denial should have been shed like a snake skin. Reality should have been my new friend and alerted me to the grave dangers that lay ahead. That would eventually happen, but not at this juncture, and in time to rectify my false sense of joy.

I was full steam ahead in the next three months planning my wedding. The date was set for December 18, 2004. The church would already be decorated for Christmas, so it would save us a lot of money. While I was busy planning the wedding, he was looking for a church. Phil was now a licensed pastor, having left the steel mill, and pursued a career in ministry and was looking for his first appointment as a pastor in a fundamental denomination. I was excited for him. This is something that he had always wanted to do even when I first met him in 1995. I wanted to support him and help make his dream come true. I had no doubt that I would be the perfect pastor's wife. I had a gifted singing voice. I was good with people and had taught Sunday school in the past. I could taste and smell a hap-pily-ever-after ending to this story. No price was too high to pay at this point. I would give up everything for "my man." He did not have to worry about me leaving him again. My commitment was full and complete. May I also add, a little bit stupid? I'd given up myself, to have what I wanted (or what I felt I **needed**), but that realization would come much later.

I threw myself into this new life. There was so much to do, and things moved at a whirlwind pace. When I look back now, I have no idea how I did it. Now it looks near impossible. That seems to be a thread in my story, where I meet a challenge and then. against what appears to be insurmount-able odds. I persevere, only to surprise myself. I find it difficult to recall and express exactly how it went down, but let me try.

About a month after we got engaged, he had an interview for a job at a church in northern Pennsylvania. I went with him. The church was small, nestled in a little town up against a beautiful mountain backdrop. I was enthralled! I could picture myself living here. What a great adventure!

I was more than ready. They called about a week later and offered him the job. With my excitement and encouragement, he accepted. He would start January 1, 2005. Now things got crazy. We had two months to sell both our homes, get married, and move to a brand-new town four hours away. We would be starting new jobs and knew no one there yet. We both were stressed to the max. We still worked full-time, packed, cleaned, and showed off our homes to prospective buyers. On Fridays, after long work weeks, I would head over to his house for the weekend. He was a very messy person and his house was a disaster area. I worked so hard trying to make sense of the place. It was very difficult at times because he was attached to his stuff and did not want to get rid of it. I was exhausted and anger was beginning to rise to the surface. I stuffed it back down, smiled, and continued on. I had no energy left to fight with him. I usually left Harrisburg late Sunday night to get home for work Monday morning. Today, as I write and remember, I am wondering where everyone was. I wish somebody would have nudged me to wake me up. "What do you think you are doing?" would also have been appropriate.

Anyway, my home was in the middle of a college town and sold about two weeks from the time it was listed. This took me off-guard. I had to move out into a rental place not much bigger than a large motel room. I stored the rest of my furniture in Phil's garage. The settlement on my home was a few days before Thanksgiving. I got the full asking price, which was a huge blessing. I made $23,000 cash, when all was said and done. I opened a savings account and put it in. I was thrilled and told one of my coworkers about how much money I had made from the sale of my home. I clearly remember her comment. She reminded me that, because it was a month before my wedding, it was my money. She told me not to add it in the marital assets but to keep it separate just in case the marriage did not last. I totally did not appreciate that viewpoint at the time. Years later my memory was jogged and her advice became one of the many lifesaving devices God provided for me in my desperate hours of need.

We got married in a small church. The church was beautiful, and many family members and friends had come to celebrate with us. The first hint of trouble, however, came before we even left the church. At the time, I used bad nerves and stress as my excuses. After all, Phil had been through a lot. He had already moved to northern Pennsylvania to be ready to start his new job the first of the year, while I would stay in Lancaster until the end of December to train a new person to take over my job as payroll administrator. The reception was coming to an end and we were saying goodbye to our guests. My mind shifted gears toward our honeymoon coming up. We were planning to spend a few days at the ocean in New Jersey. We had not been sexual through our two years of dating. I leaned over and whispered in his ear that I was excited to spend the night with him as husband and wife. I expected a knowing smile, wink, or something romantic. What I got, however, was a stern rebuke. I believe his exact words were "Don't talk like that here. Save it for tonight."

It wasn't so much what he said though that got me concerned as much as it was the tone of his voice. He sounded angry! I was very confused but quickly put it aside. Around seven that evening, I was very tired but happy as we headed south toward Jersey. As luck would have it, the car broke down somewhere on the turnpike. That delayed us a lot, and by the time we got to our destination, we were both exhausted, so I thought nothing of it when we did not make love the first night. I was beyond tired and collapsed into bed. The next day Phil took the car to finish having the repairs made. After that, we went out to a nice place for dinner. I noticed Phil was very quiet. I asked if anything was wrong, and he said *no*, so I let it go. Back at the hotel, he announced that he was tired and wanted to go to sleep for the night. I was a bit surprised as I assumed he felt rested by now as I did. I gave him the benefit of doubt, however, and he slept as I lay wide awake beside him for the second night of our honeymoon, feeling a little uneasy.

Well, the third night came along with the tired line again. I, however, was not about to buy into it. I decided to humor him. I told him to sleep and I will change into something more comfortable. I was confident that when he saw me in my new outfit there was no possibility of sleep. I will never forget the look I got from him when he saw me. The best way to describe it is a deer in the headlights look. He truly looked scared to death along with color draining from his face. I was traumatized by what I couldn't deny was total rejection on my honeymoon. I ran back into the bathroom and cried. I do not remember how long I stayed in there, but when I came out he was asleep. I crawled in bed beside him and quietly cried myself to sleep. I was getting a sick feeling in the pit of my stomach. The last night of our honeymoon I went to bed fully dressed. Now he said to me, "What are you doing? Let's get to it so we can go home and get to work." I complied, but the joy was gone from my heart. I tried to move on, push the fear and anguish out of my gut.

One foot in front of the other, my days dragged on as I did my duty as a pastor's wife. My survival skills of denial, stuffing my feelings, and pretending kicked in. The pain must have been intense, but honestly I do not remember to this day much of anything about the first two and a half years except one incident. We were married around six months. I suggested maybe we should go to therapy because of the problems that we were having. He screamed in anger at me. I remember his exact words to this day: "I will only go to therapy to pursue a divorce." His horrible and shocking response kept me quiet for another two years. Around September 2007, the pain became so great it overcame my denial and fear. The healthy part of me finally started to face reality. The truth of my marriage dawned on me when I read the book *The Abusive Relationship* by Patricia Evans.

I was being severely abused by my husband. Also, I was intimidated by his temper outbursts and his unexpected anger. It was wearing me down. I became suicidal for the first time in my life. I began to see my childhood flash before my eyes during that relationship with my husband. He was so much like my father! I had my father back controlling me all over again! I was in my fifties and just wanted to die. I did not want to live and face the shame and self-loathing I felt for myself. I even had a plan how I could die and make it look like an accident so my children would not have to know anything about it. I pictured myself driving on the freeway around 65 miles an hour, which was the usual speed limit, so no one would be suspicious. I would cross over into oncoming traffic. Death would come quickly and painlessly. Mourners probably would think I had fallen asleep. What a tragic accident, but life continues on, and I would be free. As I was picturing my death scene, an amazing thing happened. I can only describe it as a miracle, because it completely changed the course I was about to take. It was quick and intruded into my thoughts like a flash of lightning. It was bright and vivid with colors that took my breath away. In my mind's eye, I saw a huge body of water, a horrible storm, a boat with frightened people screaming.

"Save us!" they cried. "We are all going to die!"

Then I saw him.

Jesus!

His hands were stretched out skyward toward the storm. His words were loud and with authority.

"Peace, be still!"

There was immediate calm and bright sunshine. He turned, looked at me, and smiled. No words can really describe this correctly. The best way I can say it is I felt bathed and covered all over in pure love. I felt at peace and filled with a will to live. I was not alone. God had spoken. He was with me to help just as He had many times before.

This experience gave me the main ingredient to start the fight. It is called hope. As long as I have hope, I can make it through. Most of my feelings and struggles from here on out, I am going to take from my diary, which I started sometime after this. My battle was just beginning. I cannot trust my memory very much during this period of time. It was so painful, I blocked it all out. What I wrote down at the time in my diary is the most accurate. I do know my writing started after Phil and I entered therapy. I do not remember how I confronted him or how we ended up in therapy.

The crazy thing about abuse is how the victim is made to walk on broken glass all the time because you never know what will set him off. Who would have thought just closing a door instead of leaving it open could cause such a senseless verbal attack. That is the nature of the beast. No matter how long things are okay, you can never relax.

What I am beginning to learn is that I need to make life choices from a conscious level. The discernment has to come from the facts and knowing that person over a period of time. I am still learning not to turn red flags into green ones just because I feel passion or just not wanting to be alone. Trust me though when I say you are never more alone than when you are with an abuser. I would much rather be single with healthy relationships with girlfriends, men friends, and family than to go through what I had with Phil. If I can just help one person out there who reads this book to stay safe, reliving my nightmare will have been worth it. Until I started writing this memoir, I had no idea how hard it would be. It has been good for me, though, in the long run. It has forced me to go deeper within. I find myself paying more attention to current relationships. I am really listening to what people are saying and watching their behavior. I am uncomfortable at times, but the growth is worth it. I feel confident now that I can and will run from an abuser early on. I can never take that for granted, though, as I am a work in progress. I cannot stress enough how vital it is to recognize abusers before the feelings and emotional attachment begins. Then it is much more difficult to see clearly. The temptation is to make excuses for them. Try to explain things away in your head. I know, I have been there done that.

Another thing I want to address is a mistake that I made. If you are married and being abused, never, ever go to marriage therapy or counseling together. Go by yourself to an experienced abuse therapist. As I have said previously, in my relationship with Phil, that made the abuse escalate. This was very dangerous for me. At the time, I did not know it or understand. Now I do and can share it with you.

The abuser at this stage in the relationship is afraid of being found out. Also, there is the possibility that you will become aware and be able to escape. The sad fact is that too many therapists still have trouble recognizing abusers in therapy. I do not mean to criticize them. I am sure they do the best they can. It is hard to tell sometimes, because abusers are very good actors. They know how to behave and speak well in front of the therapist. Phil could lie, distort, and twist the facts. Then I became confused and had trouble hanging onto reality. So how does the abused really know what is going on? To keep safe, go by yourself to an abuse therapist.

Also, the abused may have trouble expressing what is really happening at home behind closed doors. They may have been warned or threatened by the abuser before therapy to say only certain things or they will pay—that is what my abuser did. There are so many hindrances to getting real help. It is not always the fault of the therapist. It puts them in a tough position. The main reason to go to therapy by yourself is that abuse is not a marriage problem. Abuse is a separate issue all by itself. That has to be addressed and dealt with before anything else. I learned the hard way. As long as it is thought to be a marriage problem, they will drag you in the mud and bury you. Trust me, I was no match for the cunning skills of an abuser. The last therapist we had tried her hardest to help us communicate, thinking that was one of our many problems. Of course, we had communication problems because an abuser does not want to connect, so there will be no real communication no matter what you do. Bless her, she tried. We were given homework to do and practice. Phil just laughed when we got home and never ever even looked at the material, let alone did any of it. So back to therapy we went, and in my ignorance I told her his reaction, that he didn't want to do any homework, and that it was not done.

He was so convincing that even the therapist got diverted. He spoke up about how busy he was trucking (he was now a truck driver) during the last two weeks, how he hated his job, how angry he was at me because I was not working at the time. So to my utter amazement, the therapist began to side with him. She asked him questions about what kind of job he would rather have. He told her that he was really a pastor and about how unfairly he was treated when getting fired by the church in the south where we had moved to. He explained how he was called by God to preach and not drive a truck. I sat there stunned as he diverted the therapist's attention away from the abuse. We never did get to the real issues of him not wanting to do the work, much less recognizing the abuse, manipulation, lying, and control.

I alone knew what went on at home and that he had no desire to improve anything. I tell you all this to show you how pointless it is to try and treat abuse as a marriage problem. It will just be a nightmare and you will lose, and I eventually did. By the time the therapist's eyes were opened to see who he really was, he knew it also. He simply stopped being nice, picked a fight with her, and blamed her for not being able or competent enough to help us. After six months of therapy, Phil refused to go back. From this experience, I learned that abuse in a relationship should not be treated as a marriage problem. Rather, the abused needs to seek private counseling. If the abuser is willing to go into therapy, all the better. But each should pursue therapy separately. Phil and I went through three different therapists to no avail, and the same predictable patterns from Phil continued. It is my hope and prayer that my experience and insights can help others avoid this trap. I know therapists try to be objective and empathic, but when there is abuse, marriage therapy doesn't work.

I had shared a segment earlier about learning to write or "journal" to help focus and gain perspective. What follows is several years of my marriage to Phil, while trying desperately to make the marriage work, including counseling outlined, which may help others focus on their situations and ascertain whether there is a real problem in a relationship of their own...

19

Dear Diary

2007

September 6, 2007

Dear Diary,

This morning was a setback for our marriage. It has been three weeks since verbal abuse. Then this morning it caught me off-guard and came again. I was just starting to feel safe and then I was hit. It was so hurtful for me and a big setback to being able to trust him. I am also angry because I do not deserve abuse. All I did was retrieve his laundry from his bedroom. I shut the door behind me. He screamed and shouted blaming "you" statements of all kinds. I really do not want to write them all down. I am sure you can imagine what they were. The crazy thing about abuse is how the victim is made to walk on broken glass all the time because you never know what will set him off. Who would have thought just closing a door versus leaving it open could cause such a senseless verbal attack. That is the nature of the beast. No matter how long things are okay, you can never relax. It was a torture chamber for me.

September 26, 2007
Dear Diary,

I got some bad news yesterday. Phil said that the only reason he is in therapy is because he is afraid that if he doesn't go I will leave him. Therapy has done him no good because he is not willing to open up his heart and learn together. I don't see a lot of hope for our marriage at this time. I pray he has a change of heart. I think I will just work on my stuff and leave him alone. There is nothing I can do if he isn't willing to do the work.

October 6, 2007
Dear Diary,

It seems like a little breakthrough in therapy last time. I think Phil got in touch with some issues involving his mom. He is projecting his feelings of anger on me that belong to his mom. Also, the lack of touching and sexual desire is very painful. He is seeing me as his mother. He really doesn't see me; he sees his mom and is completely turned off. I feel so lonely and hardly connected to him at all. I sure hope he works through the past. If he doesn't, I don't know if I will want to stay with him.

October 22, 2007
Dear Diary,

About the time I think maybe we have emotional safety, he unleashed anger on me again over something very small and not really about that issue. He makes fun of my tears, which represents my hurt. That really angers me. If by March he has not changed his attitude, I need to leave. This is not good for my health. I can do better than this. I know it will upset the fruit basket, but I need to take care of myself. Then there is the big issue about lack of physical warmth that he does not want to face. No sex or touching for seven months. No kissing, no passion, no romance or feelings. This is crazy! This is abusive. It feels like he wants to keep conflict going as an excuse not to touch me and be warm. God needs to do a miracle or it's over. I don't know what else to do.

December 8, 2007

Dear Diary,

It has been a long time since I wrote to you. To date it has just been more of the same crap with Phil. Mainly verbal abuse. He will not stop or face it. Today I decided to work toward a separation. I did not want it to come to this, but I just cannot take it anymore. I suggested we draw up an agreement as to what is acceptable in how we treat each other, but he angrily refused. This was an idea offered by our therapist. I took it from that. He wants to treat me however he wants with no boundaries. If we drew up an agreement, he would have to treat me better, but he does not want to. I am not going to stick around and be his punching bag. I do not want a divorce, but the choice is his. He must change and he flatly refuses.

December 22, 2007

Dear Diary,

Tonight Phil was putting twigs, newspaper, and a log in the fireplace to start a fire. My daughter Angie is here with us. He took the broom when done, and was sweeping up in front of the fireplace. I said to him:

"There is a dustpan and brush there if you need it."

"I will let you build a fire from now on" was his response. He was very angry.

"What's the matter?" I asked.

Again, I got another lame response. "Nothing"

After that, he behaved aloof and very distant. He seemed angry but would not talk about it. I feel shaky and taken off-guard. My emotional safety is gone again.

2008

January 8, 2008

Dear Diary,

We had another therapy session without openness and honesty from Phil. This is not doing any good at all. In fact therapy appears to be making him angrier. On the way home, he takes it out on me with verbal attacks, which we had just talked about never doing again in therapy. It is like he heard nothing and has no intention of changing anything. What a waste of time.

Therapy only works if you want help. It is pretty obvious Phil does not.
He will do anything to keep from connecting. Anger is his main intimidat-
ing weapon. I am learning though that it is not about me. I am capable of
closeness. I feel good about myself. I will not let him define me and put me
down. Here are some of the nasty things he said to me on the way home from
therapy.
"You are trying to cause problems."
I told him this is an unacceptable way of communicating with me. He ignored
me and continued on.
"You are trying to start an argument. This is all about control for you. You
are being disagreeable. Take more Xanax [an anti-anxiety medication that I
was taking at the time to help me cope with his abuse]. Put your brain in gear
before you open your mouth. I don't think this marriage is going to work."
I have asked Phil nicely not to talk to me this way many times, but he just
gets angrier. The more I protest the angrier he gets. Then he accused me
of trying to control him. This is crazy! I tell him that emotional safety is a
non-negotiable issue for me. It is a must-have. He tells me he has no idea
what I am talking about.

I just wanted to add a little side note here before the next journal entry.
Phil got a larger church with more pay in 2008. We moved to a church
in another state so he could take this position. We were there for only a
year when he got fired as pastor. I did not tell anyone what was going on
at home. There was no reason given as to why he was let go. I can only
guess that God was at work helping me to escape. Several months after he
lost his job, we moved back to Pennsylvania. He got his CDL (trucking
license). Now he was on the road and gone sometimes two or three days
at a time, which was a blessing. It allowed me time alone to get stronger
abuse-free. I was also glad because of having family and friends in the area.

February 28, 2008
Dear Diary,
Phil and I are done with therapy now. He is starting to drive a truck. After
eight months of therapy, we made no progress. Phil refuses to take any respon-
sibility for his issues. He blames me for it all. Without ownership of his stuff,

there is no way that we can make it. Also lack of trust and respect is poisoning our relationship. I feel really bad, but it takes two to make it work. If he is not willing, we cannot stay together. I do not want to settle for less than a healthy relationship. It is so painful for me to see Jennifer and Angie go through this. They have already lost their biological father and now this. I am trying to give myself grace and compassion to learn from this. Beating myself up will not be helpful in any way.

March 21, 2008
Dear Diary,
I have memories come back to me of how Phil pushed me and the kids away. Jennifer suggested we take our family pictures together. He got angry and said no. Also he would not give us any of his family pictures to hang on the wall. This is crazy stuff from him and not normal behavior at all. I talked to Dr. Haffery in therapy alone after Phil was done. His words brought me a lot of encouragement. I felt sane again. I will quote him exactly. "I have been doing this for a long time and I have never seen anyone as defensive as Phil." That was a great validation for me! There really is something seriously wrong with him!

June 14, 2008
Dear Dairy,
It has been so long since I have come here. The journey has been so painful. I had trouble even putting it into words. Phil continues to be a nightmare beyond what I could have ever imagined possible. His thinking is twisted and irrational. The verbal abuse was so traumatic for me. The other thing that sealed it for me to give up is a total lack of empathy. I can be hurting, crying, and in so much pain, but he is unmoved. Even a stranger would do better than that. Why would I want to stay married to a man like that? We had over a year of therapy in our short three-and-a-half-year marriage, and he was and is so defensive, no progress was made. In fact it made things worse because he became more abusive during that time. I deserve so much better. I am far from perfect; however, I am capable of a loving, caring relationship. At this point, I have no hope that he will change. He has no desire to explore himself. I do not want to be his scapegoat. I have a good job. God provided for my

needs. I feel happy and blessed. I am not going to try and change him. I think it is best to cut my losses and move on. I have little to nothing in common with this kind of person. God is faithful and He will see me through. I feel a loving God Who wraps His arms around me when I hurt. His love never fails! Amen!

July 7, 2008
Dear Diary,
Last Friday my daughters and I headed to Ocean Grove for three days at the shore. We had the best time ever. We talked, lay in the sun, read books, and ate wonderful food. The weather was perfect, not a cloud in the sky. We stayed in an ocean-front motel room. The place was called A House by the Sea. The three of us slept together in a king-size bed. It was so much fun. It had been many years since the three of us spent quality time together. And it was such a beautiful setting. Jennifer took lots of pictures. Also we had a great time collecting seashells. It was a time of rejuvenation, sharing memories of the past, and making new ones. It was a time of continued healing from past hurts. We shared together dreams of a bright future. God is good in taking care of us with a safe trip on the highway and in the ocean. God is the author of peace and not confusion. His will is for perfect love to cast out fear. Only His love is perfect.
On this trip I read a book titled Captivating by John Eldredge. It is very good, about the beauty of women who reflect God's beauty. God's creation is awesome in beauty! I pray that God will give me wisdom in the future choices that I make. I pray for God's will to be done on earth as it is in heaven. Amen!

August 1, 2008
Dear Diary,
Phil called a therapist. We went for the first time today. It was the same old stuff. He blames me and takes no ownership of his issues. I was so angry! I feel like it is over but he wanted to go again so I went. The therapy session came and went. I saw no change in him.
I lost my job this week at Northwestern Mutual Financial Group. I was devastated. The recession was in full swing. Packing my bags now is put on hold

until I find a job. It is just a matter of time. I don't think after all the pain he caused me that I can ever love him again.

August 14, 2008

Dear Diary,

Phil decided to try therapy again. This is the result of our third session. It all came to the bottom line. I am so glad that the therapist cut right to the chase. She talked to the therapist that we had for eight months in the south about his experience with us. She confronted Phil with a choice to do the hard work and quit blaming me or end the relationship. So the ball is in his court. Of course, he is angry not wanting to make any of those choices. The therapist also established ground rules for therapy right up front. No blaming me. She said if he does she will call him on it every time. She is a brave woman to stand up to Phil. That was what he needed. His trying to fool me, the therapist, and everyone else is over. He has until September 1st to make a decision. So I have nothing to do but wait. It is going to be a long two weeks. I continue to pray that God will give me another good job.

August 25, 2008

Dear Diary,

We have been through a lot together. Last night Phil said he did not think that our relationship is going to make it. He is still blaming me and the thera-pist now also. Nothing changed yet!

September 4, 2008

Dear Diary,

Yet again Phil failed to take off work for therapy. It feels like he is stalling and does not want to face his issues. Of course, this is nothing new. I guess I still have hope but very little at this point. The therapist wants him to just answer one question: "Do you want to do the hard work that it takes for this marriage to work?"

She wants introspection from him without blaming me as a way of escape. I am prepared to leave him at this point if he decides that he does not want to work. He is too damaged to have a healthy marriage, which is what I want. Emotional health is very important to me. I shed a lot of blood, sweat, and tears for my own. I need a partner willing to do the same. If we don't have the same heart and soul, I don't want to continue. I want to work hard at dealing with my own issues right now. I know God is taking care of me. This is not my fault. I am and always have been willing to do my part, which is a lifelong pursuit. A few days ago, I heard God say it is okay to let go of Phil. I am not a failure. There are no mistakes in life, only lessons to be learned. I know that I will grow through this experience. I would not have wanted to go through so much pain to learn but I guess that is the nature of life. I want to work and nurture myself during this difficult and challenging time. God is loving and good. He will never leave me no matter what. That is the security I need for the rest of my life. I will work hard on loving myself the way God does. His word is life and health to all my flesh!

October 24, 2008
Dear Diary,
Phil said twice today in therapy that he wants a divorce. I am so heartbro-ken. Even though he has made a decision like we asked him to, I was still hoping for a miracle. I am very sad right now. I gave up so much for him in Lancaster, Pa. I gave up a good job and sold my beautiful townhouse that I had bought. In the last four years, we have moved all over the place. I would have supported him and loved him forever if he loved me. I am seeing now that he never did love me. He cannot because he does not love himself. He has so much self-hatred and shame. It appears he failed to face his past abuse as a child by his parents. His mother had bipolar disorder and drank. His father was mean and drank also. He was the oldest one and had to grow up too fast. He cooked for his two younger brothers and a sister. I more than anyone understand what he went through. I would have stayed with him and helped him heal if only that would have been his desire. He wanted to run away, which many people resort to who carry so much pain from their childhood. There is an old saying that you can run but not hide. That is so true. Without healing your past will always break through to the surface. All I can do now is trust God for my future. He will take care of me somehow, someway. The walk of faith is really hard. But many people of God before me have done it and I can too. God is faithful and will make a way when there seems to be none.

2009

January 13, 2009
Dear Diary,

I decided to go to Certified Nurs[ing] A[ssistant] training. Jobs are getting so difficult to find as the recession is now very serious with many people out of work. I feel like I can still find a job in the health care field.

January 15, 2009
Dear Diary,

I feel like living with Phil I am losing my grip on reality. I feel in a dreamlike state. I fear that I am losing my mind and going insane. My thoughts are very troubled and jumbled. I have never felt this way before. I need help, but I do not know who to go to? Who can help me? I feel like screaming at the top of my lungs and then crying until my eyes are dry. What is really going on? I hate to say it but it feels like pure evil, lies, and deception going on all around me at home with Phil. I do not feel it when I am away from him. What is this? I need some answers! I feel nervous and tense, unable to relax. There is no safe emotional climate. How long can I go on without getting relief? I have trouble concentrating. I have trouble trusting my perceptions, intuition, and feelings. It is very frightening to lose a grip on what is real or what is imagined. I have never been here before. It feels like something about Phil is really harming me!

Between this letter and the next, I wrote the letter you saw in Chapter 9.

August 5, 2009
Dear Diary,

I have been busy adjusting to my new home. It has been a little over two months now since I left Phil. I bought a small mobile home in a beautiful park. I can feel the healing coming more each day as I am in a safe emotional environment. I met with Pete, who is a friend that came into my life recently. He is going to paint my new home. I am excited about that. Right now it is a baby blue on the outside, which I don't like. I am going with a nice beige color.

The last few weeks I have been so hungry. It is a spiritual hunger and thirst. My soul cries out for God. I can identify with David in Psalm 42:1–2 where he says: "My soul pants for you, O God." I am thirsty for the well of living water that never runs dry.

I feel a deep stirring like an underground volcano wanting to erupt, burst forth with beauty and power. God is doing something in my heart. I am not sure what it is, yet I do know. I have trouble putting it in words. I try to pray but all that comes is a deep groaning and yearning that I have not felt in a long, long time. It feels like an awakening from the dead. It is my heart awakening! I believe being away from Phil has allowed the real me to surface. It feels like passion under a full moon with the love of my life. He is my soul mate. God Himself is standing before me biding me to come to Him, walking on the water. I am hearing His voice to step out of the boat. I am here and will not let you sink. Take my hand. I will help you walk by faith and not by sight. He is healing me, spirit, soul, and body. I am excited to see what God has planned for me. His best is what I seek. The anointing is what breaks the yoke of bondage.

November 14, 2009

Dear Diary,

Phil has made no effort to come up with a plan to reconcile. Everything I suggest he turns down. I wanted us to go to a program run by Phil Haven Hospital outpatient unit. It is called Recovery of Hope. It is designed for couples like us who have tried it all and are ready to call it quits. It is a week of tests and intensive therapy to really get to the bottom of what is going on. I should not have been surprised when Phil refused to do this. He does not want a solution. At this point I feel done with him unless I see a real change. Meanwhile I am enjoying my youngest daughter Angie living with me for a year. What a blessing she is. She is a beautiful woman and a joy to have around! She just bought a new Honda Civic, which she is very happy with. The price of gas is so high and this car does very good on gas mileage. She is moving out after a year to accept a job in Massachusetts. I am very proud of her getting a great job right out of college with a master's degree. I know she will do well in her life.

20

Blame and Grace

It is May 2012, and I am recalling my thoughts and feelings from the woman's meeting I went to back in April 2009, which you have read in my diary entry shown in Chapter 9. It is still very encouraging.

Alone we die. With connection we live. We must have a relationship with God and others to live to the fullest, which is God's desire for us all. Our inner critic is the loudest. It is the hardest to forgive ourselves and silence this inner monster. I learned that life is sometimes hard but God is always good. I want to use my story for God's glory. Then God's glory becomes my story. I believe this is His will in all our lives.

Blame is an indication of some deep pain. We blame so many things on so many people. Sometimes I feel as though the blame should be directed toward me. I blamed God, myself, my pastor, and my husband. There are, of course, many other things to blame as well. We need healing that only God can provide deep in our soul where the wounding occurred. When we have self-hatred we begin to die. The great tragedy is what dies inside of us while we live. If we have shame deep inside us, it causes shameful behavior. Without healing, we look into our past with resentment and blame. We live today angry and we face the future with fear. This is me right now. I feel hopeful after today to be able to accept grace and forgiveness and move on. We cannot control anyone but ourselves. The pain, along with shame and blame, are all a path to nowhere. We do desperate things when we are in pain. The only way to heal is to accept God's grace and forgiveness. Grace is free; all we need to do is receive it. The price was paid by Jesus on the cross when He uttered "It is finished"; it remains finished. We cannot add or take away anything from that. It is always sad to God when we do not accept the high price He has paid and we attempt on our own to continue to pay. It breaks His heart because He loves us so much! We are his dear children. His desire for us is freedom, not bondage. The enemy comes to steal, kill, and destroy. Jesus came that we might have life and have it more abundantly.

Trauma changed me forever here on this earth. To talk about it helps me make the necessary changes to heal. I must break the silence. When I do, the stronghold is broken. I want to be honest with myself and others. When it is brought out into the light, the darkness flees. That is why Jesus proclaimed that we are the light of the world. He wants us to shine bright for Him. Forgiveness is a long, long journey. The need to punish myself is saying that Jesus did not do enough on the cross. The truth is that our past, our present, and our future sins are totally paid for. What a hard reality for most of us to absorb and practice. Jesus suffered so I do not have to. I can let myself out of prison and go free. God saw me and knew my total life before I was born. He knew what decisions I would make or not make. I am not a surprise to Him. He has a special purpose and plan for you and me. I am an amazing person because of Jesus. God's plan is greater than I could ever think of. I am still a work in progress. We all are. While in pain, my eyes have seen Jesus. I will allow freedom, peace, and joy into my heart. I make a choice to agree with God and release the need to punish myself.

21
Regaining Control

I now realize that everything about Phil and our relationship was harmful to me. Many of the things I ignored in the rekindled relationship with Phil were due to things operating in my own life—fears of failing health and projections about aloneness that led me to put on blinders and not see what was ahead of me. It was more difficult to see it up close when I was in the thick of it. When we lack confidence and love for ourselves, we project a victim or "prey" mentality in how we ignore or tolerate small abuses. This feeds the abuser, it's all they need to know. The abuser knows exactly what to do to control his "victim." This amounts to brainwashing and is meant to weaken you and isolate you so that in the end you are unable to escape. That is how an abuser controls their victim, even if they are not consciously aware that is the abuser's process. It is making you dependent on them in every way. The abuser wants to reduce you to feeling you need them to survive. This gives them security that you will never leave, which I think is their greatest fear, due to their own brokenness. Thank God I was one of the lucky ones. I was healthy enough to escape after four years in an abusive marriage. The sad news, however, is that there are many who never do. Some get away only to be stalked or killed. Abuse of any kind is very dangerous and is to be taken seriously!

One of the highest-risk groups in my opinion are women who have been abused as a child in their family of origin like me. I believe this in part because "normal" and "healthy" have not been modeled for them. So in my case, I could only guess what was or should have been normal. In my experience, a relationship could be abusive, but if it was better than what I had in childhood, I did not even see it or recognize the abuse. To a normal person, it would have felt really bad, or just off-center or "wrong," but to me it was okay and felt what I supposed was normal. Couple that with my own need for validation by being "partnered" and I was already set up to put up with a lot to have "connection." For those in high-risk groups, like me, the goal is to grow, educate yourself, and continue to heal, read books, and pray.

Many abusers have been perfecting their control of others for some time. They most likely were abusive before you entered the picture. This was true with Phil. I was his third wife. The two before me had left him. The first wife left after five years of marriage. The second wife left him after 13. I have never spoken to her personally. I did hear from his daughter before we married that in her opinion her mother was abused. I just dismissed it at the time as mother and daughter sticking together. It did not dawn on me until years later that she may have been trying to warn me about him.

As I said, I was able to get away after just four years. They appear to me as wasted years. In some ways they were. In other ways I learned some valuable lessons and insights. I am not perfect and never will be. I do know, though, that I will never be as naïve and unconscious in my choice of a partner as I was in 2004.

By 2012, eight years later, I had become very picky when it came to relationships and intimacy. My soul was protected and in a safe place. At the same time, I had not gotten bitter or unable to love, if and when the real thing should come along. The key here was being content to wait for the real thing, as opposed to acting out of desperation or the fear of being alone. Fear and denial cost me dearly and are things I do not want to repeat. I recognize that they were survival mechanisms in my childhood but that, as an adult, they are deadly traps! What I am about to share with you was not in my conscious mind at the time I was going through it. If I were aware, I would have made very different decisions. This awareness came to me over time and in therapy after my divorce from Phil.

22

Looking Backward
to Look Forward

What I'm about to share may have had a huge subconscious impact on driving me to enter into a relationship so as not to face this potential issue alone. In 2002 I started having episodes of out-of-control fear one day at work. It all started as I noticed some memory problems. I had trouble spelling easy routine words. My mind at times seemed to just stop and go blank. I had not noticed or felt anything like this before. My coworkers let me know that I was making more mistakes than usual for having done this job for eight years and I was known for being meticulous and accurate with payroll by this time and normally made very few errors. What was happening?

I began to worry that something very serious was wrong with me. I was healthy most of my life. Now I was single and alone. My symptoms became worse over the next few months. I also started to have involuntary muscle spasms in my right foot, curling my toes under. These were painful and kept me awake at night. I decided to go to the doctor. He was concerned enough to send me for an MRI. This test revealed a small lesion in the central nervous system—my brain. The doctor said it looked consistent to him with a multiple sclerosis (MS) lesion. However, he could not give me that diagnosis because there was only one lesion and, as the name suggests, an MS diagnosis requires multiple lesions.

I assumed the worst immediately. I jumped right to the fact that it was just a matter of time until another lesion appeared and I would get the dreaded MS diagnosis. Now I was facing something totally new and foreign to me. This was when I pictured my future alone with MS and no one to take care of me. It was the beginning of 2002, about the same time that Phil and I had started dating again.

I had my first panic attack. I called up Phil and managed to feel a little relief. It did not last long, though. Fear and panic dug their roots deep in my heart. The root of it was not only fear of the disease but mostly of facing it alone. I did not tell my daughters, because they had just lost their father in 1999. I did not want them to worry about me or be afraid of losing me also, or having to care for an invalid mother. I wanted to protect them from any more pain.

Nevertheless it felt like I was falling, falling really fast from 30,000 feet without a parachute. I also had nightmares and dreams of being in the ocean thousands of miles from land. The waves were huge and I was sinking with no life raft. I woke up in a sweat, screaming for help. I now believe that Phil became my self-perceived life raft and my parachute. In the coming five years, I would have an MRI every six months, looking for another lesion to confirm the diagnosis. So now you can see why I was not going to let go of Phil no matter what. The fear and desperation had frozen me in place. I chose to let denial rule unchallenged. I did not see what possibly lay ahead. I focused on how wonderful our time had been dating five years earlier and ignored all the current data. I was immersed in my survival mode from childhood when I was abused, threatened, and afraid. My motivations and decisions were made out of desperation not to be alone when I got the possible MS diagnosis. The irony of it all is that I do not have MS. No other lesions ever showed up after five years, and I stopped having regular MRI scans. The diagnosis was something similar to restless leg syndrome. I take a muscle relaxer at night now and Tylenol PM to sleep. The doctors do not know how or when the one lesion got there, but it is harmless. Who knows how that lesion appeared? At this point no one cares, including me. The doctors do not want to see me as long as I feel healthy. At 61 years old, I feel good! I play volleyball once a week, go on regular walks, and hike.

23

Continuing to Learn

I have found in my research, counseling, and learning prior to writing about my own abuse that there is an alarming lack of awareness of what abuse is really all about. I think our courts, laws, preachers, counselors, therapists, whatever, are truly unaware of the tremendous power of verbal and emotional abuse. I might also add that abuse is not gender-based. I think, when it comes to physical abuse, that tends to be more from men. In my opinion, if a man were being physically or otherwise abused by a woman, it would go largely unreported. I personally have had no firsthand experience with women abusers, but I have talked with a few men that I know who were abused by women.

It appears that the major focus is on physical abuse, which is much clearer, and some emotional abuse victims claim they'd rather be beaten than demeaned constantly. At least everyone seems to be on the same page with physical abuse. Lots of help is available, including the police, shelters, and protection from abuse orders. I do not want to minimize physical abuse in any way; it is horrible! But somehow it gives substance to abuse, whereas verbal and emotional abuse is harder to document. My therapist told me that in her practice many abusers started out with verbal and emotional abuse and ended up escalating to physical abuse. She also added that any kind of abuse continues to worsen in time if not addressed and stopped. Just remember: if you are hit once, you most likely will get hit again and again in spite of numerous apologies and promises. Take it very seriously the first time abuse of any kind happens and get help!

Tell your abuser to stop it and not to do it again. Now that seems clear enough; however, true abusers, once alerted to their hurtful behavior, not only do not stop it, they often do it more. Verbal and emotional abuse becomes more effective over time as it wears down the victim's sense of self-esteem and self-worth, which not only destroys the relationship but leaves deep emotional wounds that do not heal easily.

I know firsthand because this is what Phil did to me. I am still working to recover my self-esteem and value. Being aware of such indicators of abusive behavior early in a relationship may prevent much pain and heartache later. I wish I would have known then what I know now.

If you even suspect that you are in an abusive relationship, even if it is subtle, there will be red flags, but you still must be educated and pay attention. Listen to your intuition. People, and especially women, usually have a sixth sense about things that are "not quite right." We sometimes know, but for various reasons dismiss it. Sometimes those reasons are our own baggage, and we own that, but in the end, whether you have your own issues or not, never give another person the right to constantly and systematically abuse you and control you for their own purposes. Pay heed to the small or simple things that set off questions in your heart! When I was dating Phil, there was a situation that turned out to be a huge red flag that continued into marriage and never got resolved. If only I had had the courage, the foresight, and the confidence to have pursued it right then, I am certain that I would not have married him.

I remember this night clearly. We were engaged to be married at the time, so that is why this event disturbed me. We were at his house watching TV. A commercial came on and I snuggled closer to him and kissed him. His shirt was buttoned all the way up to the top. All I did was open the top one and run my hands over his chest. This was pretty normal for an engaged couple in love to exchange harmless intimacies that weren't of a full sexual nature. That is all I did, and turned my attention back to the TV. I would not have given it another thought had it not been his strange response.

"What did you do that for?" He then quickly buttoned his shirt again. It was not just the question that shook me so much, but his anger and tone. He was clearly irritated at being touched. This did not feel like a normal response to me. I expressed to him that his response concerned me as we were going to be married in three months.

"Is this anger at being touched going to carry over into marriage?"

It was a legitimate question to ask. I assured him that this definitely would be a problem for me in marriage. Now he became angry at the question.

"Oh, you worry too much! Everything is going to be okay."

So now my concern was dismissed, conversation over. I unwittingly had just shown Phil that this was a good way to "shut me up." Because of my own denial, I was not using our engagement to "test the waters" and see how the shoe fit, but to show Phil how to control me and keep me from dealing with all the things that were wrong, but I refused to see. Looking back, I see how in many instances I was setting myself up to be a victim. I already alluded to the fact that I thought I might develop MS and was terrified to be alone battling that. I lived in a fantasy of what it had been like with Phil five years earlier and refused to see what was unfolding in front of me. At the time, it felt as though it wasn't right, but I could not force myself to even consider that there was a flaw in this "perfect plan" I had made, so I continued to absorb hurt and rejection, acting as if it was okay, but deep inside I couldn't deny that I was being continuously wounded.

This is the point where I should not have let him or his anger intimidate me into silence. A good thing would have been to bring it up again at a later date. If I was not taken seriously again, was dismissed, this would have been a perfect time to have sought some outside counsel and done some serious inventory and evaluation. Instead I just let it go. It turns out I did not worry near enough about this situation! It turned out to be just the tip of the iceberg and the frigid waters that would be our life together. Everything was far from okay! Never let anyone intimidate you into silence. My own fears of being alone drove me to ignore what would come back to haunt me many times in the years to come.

24

More Fear
Dark Night of the Soul

Back to 2012. What is happening to me and why? Sometime in the last two months something has gone really wrong. It was not unlike a massive train wreck. I am left wondering how this could happen when I have come so far and learned so much. But here it is again the evidence of more deep wounds from the pathology of my past. I am forced along the way, kicking and screaming on the inside and crying on the outside. There is no one to talk to about what is going on and even if there was what would I say. I feel little and lost. I am aware of a terrible shudder of loneliness inside my gut. I am aware also of fear coming to the surface. Well, maybe the fear is more like stark terror! I try not to let myself feel it because it threatens to swallow me and I will cease to exist. Yet I must struggle as I have in the past to figure out what might be going on. I pray, pray, and pray some more in desperation for answers. I have more trouble sleeping. I dream sometimes about not being able to wake up. I feel relief, then disappointment when I do wake up. I eat but it tastes like cardboard. I want my dad to hold me, tell me he loves me and everything will be okay. "Wait a minute!" says my anger that follows right after I sense wanting my dad to hold me. He is the reason for this pain. Then I feel the hatred for a few seconds all over again. I groan knowing that I am in the victim role. The hard work to overcome is mine, even though the damage was done so many years ago by Dad. I start to accept the fact that no one can rescue me, just as it was up to me when I was 19 years old. I suddenly feel very tired. Maybe at 61 years old I can still get healthier and learn. I steel myself for the recurrent battle ahead.

One little piece of it at a time. That is how the insight and awareness started. I had one thought that seemed to make sense and bring me some peace. I see the integration that needs to happen now. My head and my heart are so fragmented. It is my healthy true self wanting to burst forth with new life. I can almost see these last two months as a good thing. I see that the recurring challenges are needed, because if I am not forced to grow, I will not choose the effort required to grow on my own. As the Bible says, when a seed is put in the ground, it dies, but new life springs up with such beauty that we forget the sacrifice the seed made. I am beginning to feel something similar to hope! I feel that tingle that I can rise again above this latest obstacle. I remember hearing somewhere that what does not kill you will make you stronger. I think I will be stronger on the other side. That is my desire anyway. That has been my history.

It started out small with me telling a little white lie. I told myself shades of gray re okay. However, it was not good because the white lie became toxic and a black mark on my soul. This is the nature of lies. Lies started with Satan in the Garden of Eden, and today lies are still our downfall. If it would have just involved me, maybe I could have controlled it. However, others sometimes have a way of noticing changes in me that I do not see in myself. So someone asked me about something involving the lie I told myself and it changed everything. To my horror, I passed the lie on to them very convincingly. My head screamed, "No, tell the truth!" but my heart would not let me. Now I had crossed the line into deception. It will take more energy and deceit to keep that up. I entered into the total abandonment of myself by acting out a role that took me to hell and back. I feel terribly ill as I fight my way through this. I did not realize that I was still capable of hurting myself and others so badly before coming to my senses. It teaches me how deep and driven the subconscious wounding is and how simply fallible we as humans are without constant focus on His will. In my mind, on a conscious level, it was so clear not to go there, but I did anyway, pushed along by something that felt out of my control. Some hidden force deep within me pushed me forward. Like a puppet on a string, I continued into the fog.

This is what the lie was about. I was dating someone, but I was restless and not sure if he was the one. I met someone else and wanted to get to know him while not losing the one I had. The other guy lived in another state and was in a singing group. I told my boyfriend I was auditioning for a singing group, which he was okay with. So I lied to my boyfriend about where I was going and for what reason. He never knew I had lied to him. I did not tell him. I told myself a lie, too: that we were not really in a committed relationship or that serious, so I could do this. The lie to him was obviously wrong and caused me major guilt. I thought my cheating days were behind me, and here I was caught in it again. It has ended up not working out with either the first guy or the second. Looking back on it now, I must have felt so much shame and low self-esteem from everything that had happened, especially after my third marriage failure. This lie was magnified in my mind because of how I felt about myself. This was the hole that I dug myself into and needed to get out of. I needed to free myself from the shame and guilt of my relationship choices by being the type of person I wanted to be, by walking in the truth and the light.

The good news is that I now recognize the pattern. It starts with fear and panic on a deep level that grips me in a vise so tightly I feel I can scarcely breathe, and then it takes over my mind and being. When this panic caused by fear takes over, it obscures everything else.

The same scenario drove me to marry my third husband. I was driven by fear. I thought I had or was soon to be diagnosed with MS, because of some bizarre symptoms, and I could not think of facing life with MS alone, so I ended up in a terrible marriage without seeing all of the glaring warning signs.

It is unthinkable for it to be eight years later and here it is again! I must let my feelings surface this time to acknowledge them and heal. Thank God at least this time I caught it before I married yet again in order to avoid the terror of being alone. That is the root of what has often driven me into bad choices—the fear of being alone—and it desperately needed to be addressed.

Maybe I needed to make friends with that recurring and powerful need inside me. Perhaps I needed to realize and accept that drive that lies within me and see that feeling for what it is. I constantly tell myself and others that it's God's will for us to be joined and so then I give myself permission to have those feelings inside me. What if I were to accept that is my flaw—not that God doesn't want us connected, but that my own willful drive to shield myself from my fear of being alone is my problem. How I got here, what created that subconscious need is not as important as how I'm going to cope with handling that fear and need.

Until I love myself, as I am, with or without someone external to validate my value and worth, the search for someone else to love me is futile and will end in disaster yet again. I am running out of time. Now it needs to be faced no matter how painful it is. Trust that there is a lot of pain in me with this awareness. I want to beat myself up for this waste of time and detour around it. But unless I figure out the root cause of this driving need and fix that, I cannot take the next step in healing. The overall process is needed and good, but it feels so bad!

I am having a somewhat happy and peaceful day today. I am at work as a Certified Nursing Assistant (CNA). I do private duty, so there is a lot of downtime. My boss knows that I am writing a book. She is very supportive and lets me bring my laptop to work. What a blessing that is to get paid while I write! My role as an in-home caregiver for an elderly client means that if the chores are done, I have downtime while they nap. It's nice to have a job where I can actually utilize that downtime rather than just watch TV.

I am not totally out of the woods yet, but just knowing what I have to do has set me on a path out of the madness. I do believe that I will seek some therapy for a booster shot. I think the first thing I want to do is tell the total truth to a safe person. Maybe my best girlfriend of over 30 years would be a smart place to start. The patterns of shame and secrets have to go. I can make a conscious choice to open up the blinds and let the sun shine in. Walking in light and truth will free me from stumbling in the darkness. God guides my footsteps. In Him there is no fear. God's love is perfect and casts out my fear.

I am stubborn and will never give up the fight for health. God knew what I would face, and He will never leave me or forsake me no matter what. His unconditional love is what keeps me alive and facing each new challenge. One of my favorite verses about love in the Bible is Romans 8:35–39 ("Who shall separate us from the love of Christ? Shall trouble or hardship or persecution or famine or nakedness or danger or sword? For your sake we face death all day long; we are considered as sheep to be slaughtered. No, in all these things we are more than conquerors through him who loved us. For I am convinced that neither death nor life, neither angels nor demons, neither the present nor the future nor any powers, neither height nor depth, nor anything else in all creation, will be able to separate us from the love of God that is in Christ Jesus our Lord"). Wow! What a majestic declaration and promise from him. While I am here, indulge me in sharing one more jewel. It is Romans 9:16 ("It does not therefore depend on man's desire or effort, but on God's mercy"). It is so true that without His mercy we would all be consumed. Where would I be without the grace of God? With prayer, faith, and hard work, I can shut up my inner demons and heal! I claim my right to wholeness because that is who I really am. I agree with how God made me and what His desire is for my life.

Today I am strong, focused, and deliberate. The path is clearing before me one day at a time. I try not to think too far ahead or figure everything out. Trust is better as I continue to climb higher than I have ever been before. Higher than I thought it is possible for me to go. God is not finished with me yet. I know the journey is long, but with each step I am leaving a little bit more of my toxic past behind. I am creating a new future for myself in which I will thrive and help others along the way.

25

Facing Fear and Aloneness

Until now I really had no clue that I would feel so lost and terribly afraid without a man. I still do not know what exactly it is that I am so frightened of. The crazy thing about this is how long it has taken me to face and feel the fear. Oh, don't get me wrong; I did at times feel the tip of it. I must have known at some level that it was much deeper, because why else would I rush to fix it with a new boyfriend or husband? The thing is most of me was just on autopilot. It is like going through life half-unconscious or in a trance. Unbelievable as it sounds, I have never been by myself without a husband or boyfriend. I had some idea that they were a buffer for me not facing all of my issues and demons, but little did I know how strong a buffer they were. I was and still am driven by denial even when facing a red light. I would see the light and know that it meant stop, but denial was stronger. I even saw an 18-wheeler coming and just knew that I would get hit by running the red light. Of course, this is a big part of my childhood model. It is called let's play pretend! The lesson was that what you see and what you are experiencing is not real. Denial then became my friend to help me survive the horror. I desperately needed it back then. Now it is totally useless and baggage that needs to be kicked to the curb. I am safe now. It is okay and healthy to feel and experience reality, good or bad. This is my next step of growth. I hate every minute of it honestly at this point. I will, however, make a conscious choice to reframe it and embrace it as good and necessary. I can see it as an exciting adventure like traveling to a beautiful new country. I can take the time to enjoy all the sights, smells, and scenery that I missed while rushing from one relationship to another. It is time to explore new opportunities. I have the power inside of me to be in the driver's seat or to be driven by something else. The choice is mine. No one else can walk my path for me. I am hoping and believing that there are friends who will be my cheerleaders. They will come along beside me. When I feel faint and want to give up, I hear the words "I know you are strong! You can do it."

I feel like I have spent so many years trying to fix the cracks in my foundation. There comes a time, like now, to just tear down the old building and build a new, more solid foundation. I want it to be built on my true authentic self. Involved in this amazing journey will be getting to know who I truly am. I think to myself how wonderful it would be not to have to apologize for being honest, knowing what I like or don't like. It is okay to have an opinion or desire that is different from someone else's. I do not need permission from anyone else to be me. It seems like a simple thing if you had a healthy background. But in my case, being born looking up at the bottom, it is a huge accomplishment. Denial will no longer be in this new foundation and life that is called mine. Speaking my truth in love and accepting the truth of others is the great prize for me to work toward. I am picturing it happening. I am hoping that as I give myself permission to feel the pain, fear, and devastation of all that confronts me, something miraculous will occur. It is about human surrender, one instant of being willing to trust myself and my creator, which is as close as I will get to "lifting my eyes toward the hills, where my help comes from." Once you get clear about who you are, what you are doing, and what you are being called to do, you become powerful. As you sort through the pieces of your life story, as you sift through the rubble of what is left, your character becomes stronger. You are propelled into a higher level of responsibility for yourself, into a greater appreciation for all of the pieces of your life, and into a deeper level of accountability to God. The greatest lesson I hope to learn is that I hold the key to my freedom in the center of my being. The key is the Holy Spirit. No pathology from my past is stronger than God Himself living in me and through me. The spiritual curriculum of each life has one aim: to get us back to God. If we judge our spiritual curriculum as good or bad, right or wrong, fair or unfair, we will miss the point of the lesson, and we will repeat the class over and over until we understand that what we go through in life is the roadmap back to God. For me it is the painful but necessary process of surrendering my life into God's hands and the slow, revealing process of personal redemption. It is totally possible, whatever you or I are facing, to find peace among the broken pieces of our lives. None of us is immune to the challenges of life.

One way or another, at some point in our lives, sooner or later, there will be a test of our faith, strength, and courage. I invite you to come along on this healing journey with me. I know each of our stories is different yet the same. In our combined humanness the lessons apply in some shape and form to all of us alike. My desire in continuing to be vulnerable, exposing my faults, flaws, and stubbornness, is so that you too can find a safe place to fall. I am encouraged by reading stories of others who survived personal hardships. There are so many of us, I am not alone. When I get to the end of a book or movie about someone young dying of cancer or a long talk with a young person diagnosed with cancer, I am blessed to have been a part of their life in some way. I want you to be able to picture yourself overcoming the obstacles you face better from our shared stories. I admire your strength and determination. If you can go through that holocaust and be whole, I certainly can too.

What a joy it is to know also that this world is not our final home. We are just passing through for a short time. Heaven is our final destination.

26

Emotional Conflicts

Navigating my feelings right now (2012) is like trying to fly a 747 airplane having never even been in one. Well in a way that is true. I have never been at this place before. Aging parents are hard enough on the average family. Ours is so much more traumatic and draining. My dad just got back to the nursing home from a hospital stay. He is recovering from a massive stroke. I visited with him today and I bit my lip to fight back the tears that wanted to overtake me. I love my father and need him. I forgave him a long time ago. My feelings are still wildly swinging and difficult to tame. I can have so much closure, love, and peace for my father one minute; then, with one thought of how he is the root source of all my losses, pain, and suffering that I have had in my life, I become angry all over again. After that the predictable guilt kicks in.

He is close to 90 years old and will soon be gone. I feel the big hole in my heart enlarging. I find it hard to reconcile how I am feeling about losing him. I feel deep grief and relief at the same time. I will miss him and grieve what could have been. I sense relief also because I have worked hard and forgiven him even though I will continue to feel the effects of his abuse long after he is gone. A part of me still admires him because he has spent the last 20 years of his life trying to say in many ways how sorry he is for what he has done to me. Yet this realization does not last long, because he will never truly know what he has taken from me that can never be undone. The huge gulf between us will still always be whether he is alive here or in heaven. He is the only father I have and will ever have, for better or, in this case, for worse. I continue to struggle and fear that my dad will never die. I don't mean physically, but inside of me. Will I still look for him and find him in the men I date, or the man I eventually marry again someday? Will they have the positive side of my dad that is social, friendly, with a sense of humor and a winning smile? Or will the horror of subtle abuse show up mixed with bizarre mental heath issues? Or will someone come to me who is more like my mother—totally passive, emotionally numb, being victimized by life and depressed most of the time? Or perhaps the positive side of Mom that loved God, trusted, persevered, and prayed for her children every day? Probably a buffet mixed with it all. Is there still time for me to be healthy enough to mutate their influence in me? I still hope so! I am becoming a prayer warrior, never giving up. I don't know the total answer yet. All of this is yet ahead of me. There are days I face the future with joy and confidence, sure that the worst is behind me. Days or months later, I am not feeling all that warm and fuzzy about it. I enter into the realm of fear, trembling, and anxiously waiting. I am waiting for the phone call signaling the end and the beginning. It will be both, ushering in a new normal.

For so many years our aging parents have brought us together and have been the focus of the whole family. What will we talk about when they are gone? Maybe our own mortality will come into sharper focus. I know I feel this already. The need to let my daughters know my desires as I age can fill me with dread. The pain of loss that they will feel when I am gone is depressing. However you look at it, birth, life, and death are the cycle until Jesus returns to this earth to end it all. This is my source of joy flowing like a refreshing river deep inside my soul. Without knowing this, I would be totally miserable and beyond any hope. In case you have missed it earlier in my book, this world is not meant to be forever. Heaven is forever and our final home.

27

Riding the Roller Coaster
(November 23, 2012)

I was crying and trying to accept the end. My dad had another major stroke. The nursing staff did not feel that he would survive this one. For around three days, he was in and out of consciousness. He was not able to swallow liquid or eat. We discussed as a family that Dad would not want a feeding tube or anything heroic. The quality of his life was the most important to him. I let family and friends know that the end was near. I was comforted that they would lift me up in prayer for strength to face his death. My brother Darrell had been with him for three hours holding his hand and giving him reassurance that everything is okay. As far as Darrell and others thought, he would be dying very soon. I was deep in grief trying to remember the last time I saw him and told him I loved him. I was dreading the agonizing process ahead. Then my phone rang. Darrell said, "Ruth you will not believe what happened last night. Dad suddenly woke up! He asked if Mom was still alive. I told him that yes she was. Twice he asked if she was alive and Darrell said yes. Then Dad said he was thirsty." My brother, now in shock, ran to get a nurse. She brought him a glass of apple juice. He drank the whole glass full without stopping. Then Dad said he was still thirsty. A glass of water was brought to him. He downed that also. He expressed a desire to see other family members. What a stunning miracle! God is still in control of his life and the timing of his death. This morning he ate a good breakfast and then lunch. He always liked sugar, and he told me today that the chocolate cake was the best part of lunch. Dad is back! He knew me today and was happy to see me. He shouted to everyone who would listen that I was Ruth, his oldest daughter. It was so nice to see him smile. Now it is late afternoon and I am at work as I write this. The mixed feelings are coming again. While it is great to have my dad back, I feel sad because I was ready to let go. All prepared for the end, knowing for sure this time. I feel the trauma of sudden, unexpected change again. I am on edge not knowing how long this will last before another stroke will occur from the massive blocked artery in his neck. I do not want to do this. I have no choice in the matter. The roller coaster will not stop for me. I cannot get off until the end of the ride. I thought it was the end but not yet. I am exhausted and not breathing deeply enough. I tell myself to stay calm, relax, and breathe. I will cycle this way again and need to be strong.

Mom is also nearing the end of her life on earth. She is weak, frail, and not eating much of anything. I got word today that her breathing is becoming labored. Hospice is helping my sister know when and how much morphine to give her. I am glad because I cannot stand to think that she is suffering or in pain. She has had a terribly rough life and deserves to be comfortable. Her body is worn out, but her spirit is strong. I know that to be absent from the body is to be present with the Lord. I am sure that she is ready to be in the arms of Jesus. I am trying to prepare myself to live without her. It is a big struggle. I really had no idea how painful all of this would be. I guess I figured that, because of all the abuse suffered at the hands of my parents, their deaths would not affect me much. I was so wrong! I worked hard to love and forgive them. Now I know just how much healing was achieved. I got so much closer to them than I imagined was ever possible.

I well remember the struggle I went through about 10 years ago. That was the beginning of being able to tell my mom that I loved her. What a major breakthrough for me. I established a habit of calling them both at the farm house every Sunday. Oh how happy this made them! Dad and Mom told me how much they looked forward to my call every week. I always ended it with telling them how much I loved them. I also promised to call them again on Sunday. This went on for many years. As I look back and reflect, I have no regrets in the healing process. I needed to do it for me. Even in the pain there is joy. The joy of the Lord is my strength. We will all be together again someday in heaven. Meantime the process continues. God is good and will see me through.

Eight-thirty this evening I got a text update on Mom from my sister, Jane. I quote it here for you. "Dad and she must have an unexplainable bond. Mom is still extremely frail, but she perked up a bit today. She had better intake of food and fluid." However, it puts me on a stressful emotional roller coaster, trying to adjust to all these ups and downs. I am glad they rebounded some, but then I dread the sudden drop down. All we can do is keep going day by day.

I stopped in to see Dad also tonight. What a big difference from yesterday! Only the Lord knows, but I am convinced that they are tied together. If Mom goes, Dad will too. Dad asked me tonight if Mom died. Wow! He expressed so well what I am feeling. Having been married for over 65 years, their spirits are communicating with each other even though apart. I had not even told Dad or Jane how I feel and that I am writing it in my book. What an amazing same-day rally! It encouraged me knowing that I am not alone. We are all in this together as a family. We are connected also with an invisible bond as sisters and brothers. No matter what we have been through, blood is still thicker than water, as the saying goes. I try not to think too far ahead. There is no way I can be totally prepared for their deaths. Living in the present one day at a time is the best way to do it. This is so much easier said than done, but we all strive to this end. "Therefore, do not worry about tomorrow, for tomorrow will worry about itself. Each day has enough trouble of its own" (Matthew 6:34). We can triumph over the wild ride together and be okay!

28

The Edge of a Cliff

Life is hard; God is good. This is my lifeline right now. I feel like I am standing on the edge of a cliff. I am looking down, but I don't for long. I have the fear of falling. It is too far down, and if I let myself slip, there is no way back up to the top of the cliff. I will get hurt; too much pain down there. At least I am still standing and fighting for mental health. I feel so desperate for God to intervene on my behalf. I know the many miracles I have had in the past. I need another one! I pray a lot and ask. Many verses help refresh my mind and help keep me sane. In all my ways, I acknowledge God, and He promises to direct my path. He said He would keep me in perfect peace if my mind stayed on Him (Isaiah 26:3). I must "lean not on my own understanding" (Proverbs 3:5), which to me is a great relief, because I have none right now. It feels like, as I age, there is a cumulative effect of the many years of grief, loss, and trauma. It is difficult to find a place of rest and stability. I have trouble picturing myself being single, yet now I have no energy even to date or start a new relationship. I dread my aloneness, but it is probably the best thing for me now to learn to handle.

I need to let go of the control in my life and let God bring his will into mine. I always want to feel like I am in control, but I am getting the revelation that we never really are. That is only an illusion made up to decrease our worry. Giving up that false belief is the only way to truly be in a place of peace. God is the only one in total control of our lives. It is a full-time job right now to figure out what I need to do to take care of myself. The battle is in my mind: "Be still and know that I am God" (Psalm 46:10). To hear his voice clearly and feel the divine presence makes me feel less anxious. My prayer and tears to him: Lord, help me to reframe the way I think and see things. What do you want me to learn and see? I feel so lost and needy. I've mostly viewed my singleness as a very negative state to be in. I know for sure this attitude needs to change. What if I saw this differently? How do I make my life as a single woman positive and happy? Well, this is my challenge now. I hear only one word coming to me from my pit of despair. It is *adventure*! I don't know exactly what it means or what it looks like but it is enough. Even one word is great when I am teetering on the edge. I chose to believe that it is from God. He will continue to give me more and transform my way of thinking and behaving into his. He is the potter and I am the clay. The clay has to yield to the potter's hands. Only then will the vessel be fit for its intended use. I have so much yet to learn. I am arriving at a new place with my Father. I will soon learn what a perfect Father wants to give to his children. I can sense God working in me to open up my eyes to the truth of my being. To be honest, sometimes I want to quit, but I know that is not an option for me. I am homesick for heaven. That is okay because it will be my real home someday but not yet. As long as I am on this earth, God wants me to find a way through the rocky road called life.

I would love to get past my issues for a change and help someone else. The world we live in today can be a hostile place. There are many who need a kind word, smile, encouragement. I do know that I heard God's direction to write this book. I believe that from sharing my struggles with others I will gain strength to press on. So I say it to myself and to you as many times as I need to. Life can and does get very hard, but God is love. He has good plans in store for me and you. "They that wait upon the Lord shall renew their strength. They shall run and not be weary. They shall walk and not faint" (Isaiah 40:31). Oh, how I need His words of life every day, every hour.

29

Death and Life
(December 10, 2012)

My mother passed away today. She is with Jesus Whom she loved so much. She will be missed by my family and me. I am sad for me but happy for her. I am sure she has already heard the words, "Well done, thou good and faithful servant. Enter into your reward that has been prepared for you from the beginning of time" (Matthew 25.23).

I love you Mom!

Last night when I got word from my sister Jane that Mom was dying, I was at work. I called and arranged to get off early. I usually work the 3 to 11 p.m. shift as a CNA. I left at 8:30 and got to Mom around 9 p.m. My first thought when I saw her was that even as she lay dying, she was still beautiful. She had no wrinkles in her face. Her snow-white hair was long and neatly braided, and one braid lay along each side of her neck. I stroked her hair gently and told her that I loved her. I thanked her for her continuous prayers for her 10 children. I am sure that I would not have survived without her bathing me in prayer through the years. She never quit, and her love endured through a very hard life. I sang to her. I lay my hand on her chest to feel her heart beating strong. She was soft and warm.

I stayed until almost midnight. That was the last time I saw her alive. The next day, around 1:30 p.m., the call came that she was gone.

Yes, finally the roller coaster stopped for me with Mom. I am thankful to still have my dad. Another ride will come. This is round one with losing parents. Death is so sad, so final, at least for now. It is the end of life in the body as we know it. Death is the last enemy to be destroyed in God's plan for us. When my mother's spirit left her body in what we call death, it was also the beginning of a new life. She is really not dead but alive in a new way and form. As Paul said (2 Corinthians 5:8), we would rather be absent from the body and present with the Lord. That is where my precious mother is now. She is sitting at his feet singing and worshiping. Then on her feet dancing! She is free at last from her 91-year-old body that has been worn out. My dad said it well today through his tears as I told him of her passing. He said we only die once then live forever with the Lord. How wonderful—only once we are separated, then no more! He encouraged me with those words, and my tears flowed as I held his hand in that nursing home. It was just the two of us trying to process our grief. Married over 65 years, it will be very hard on Dad. He lived to see her almost every day for the last four years. God did so much healing between them and our family during this time. It truly is another miracle as I reflect on God and his ways. "He does exceedingly, abundantly above all that I could ask or think" (Ephesians 3:20). I never would have imagined I would ever hear or see any love between them, but we brothers and sisters all did; I did. How amazing, patient, loving, and forgiving God is to us. It is never too late to learn the ways of love! God is love. Those who do not love do not know God because He *is* love! I am seeking him as never before. I need his unconditional love and forgiveness. I long for my final home. It makes me homesick, but I know God still has work for me to do here. When my time is up, I want to hear "well done" also: that I have fought a good fight and have kept the faith, and therefore Christ will give me a crown of righteousness on that day. Through my grief, in the following months and years, I will choose to praise my Redeemer. Because He lives, I live also!

30

A Stressful Funeral

I witnessed firsthand that stress and grief bring out the best and worst in a family. The same is true for all people in general, I suppose. At my mother's funeral, this certainly played out with all the chaos and drama of a soap opera. It was not anyone's fault in particular or a desire to hurt. Everyone experienced grief differently and had many needs and expectations. I just want to say that this is only my viewpoint and how I felt at the funeral. I am sure that other family members had different feelings from mine. We are all unique and yet the same. We all needed comfort but sought it out in different ways. We needed to feel safe, but that can be hard to attain at a time like this. So we all plunged forward without communicating with each other or expressing needs that many may not even have known they had. Needless to say, it did produce some conflict. As you all now know, with my family background, we all tried to survive the best we knew how.

I personally had a very difficult time. It was not just grief but all the other people who showed up for the funeral that I struggled with big time. There were two ex-spouses of immediate family members. I felt my privacy and safe place erode in one glance as I saw them coming in the line. The

163

toughest one was an ex-boyfriend who, we all knew, had been a cheater, liar, and an abuser to the women who dated him. I felt horror and disdain. Likely my reaction was heightened by some of my own marital and dating experiences, but I felt it was in poor taste to have them suddenly appear.

Then there was my mother's sister-in-law who had never visited Mom once in the four years that she was sick. She came breezing in all smiles. I had a nauseous feeling in the pit of my stomach. My throat tightened and I fought to smile and say "Thank you for coming," which was the expected response. In my heart I wish she had not come. I personally had not seen her in 20 years. Person after person from long years ago wanted to visit and talk. Too many people rushed up to me smiling and asking brightly, "How are you doing?" I was nice and stayed composed. What I wanted to say, with a nasty tone, was, "How do you think I am doing? Do you really need to ask that question? Should not the scene speak for itself? I am standing at the foot of my deceased mother's casket! How would you feel?" At times I felt like, if one more person asked me that, I would flee to the nearest exit and head for home. I prayed a lot in that line. Thankfully I made it through what to me was a very unexpected and unprepared-for experience. However, now I have a clear plan for what I want and do not want at my own funeral. I do not want my children ever to go through what I did. I only want the people who were in my life when I was alive to be invited to such a private and final event. I am going to express this to my two beautiful daughters and also put it in writing. I want invitation-only at my graduation service! There is enough grief and loss without others running interference.

I was struggling to keep my already frazzled emotions in check. The grief was overwhelming, and there was no safe place to show anything but strength. As I write this, it is a week behind me. I felt too volatile to share until I could get a sense of healing and perspective on it.

Let me say again at the end of this chapter what I said at the beginning, lest I be misunderstood. This was my experience only and how I remember it. I did not elicit any responses from other family members, nor do I blame anyone. God is my refuge and strength. He is an ever present help in time of trouble. I will look to him for my healing. I know for certain that I will see my mother in heaven again some great day. I do not grieve as those who have no hope. This is the best and final truth to hang onto.

The same day of my mother's funeral, late in the evening, I got a call from my daughter that her grandfather on her dad's side had passed away. I wept for myself and for my children as a wave of remembrance hit me from their father passing away suddenly at 47 years old. My ex-husband's death was a difficult time for me. The pain from Dan's father's passing was hard, but as I hugged my children, we comforted each other. No words were needed. We connected in a knowing, healing way that only mother and daughters can. I felt better and supported them as they attended his funeral and said goodbye for now. He too is in heaven and enjoying the presence of eternal peace and life everlasting. He was 94 years old. He really had been looking forward to seeing his wife, who had passed away two years before. Also his only son, my ex-husband, awaited his arrival in heaven. What dancing and singing there must have been! Like the song by Mercy Me called "I Can Only Imagine." I am sure the full joys of heaven are hidden from us on purpose by an all-knowing God. The gulf between life and death is intentional. I personally believe that if we knew totally what was on the other side, it would be impossible to live anymore on the earth. I've heard others say that if we saw what lies ahead, everyone would be believers and there would be no purpose for faith. Those who have experienced near death and got a glimpse of heaven have trouble with reentry to this world and its trials, pain, and challenges. Most, if not all, are so upset that they had to return to their bodies and earth. They have done their best to encourage others from their brief experience on "the other side." It is the only reason it seems that they were not allowed to enter heaven just yet. God was not finished with them here. Their message needs to be heard. More souls need to get saved and escape hell. God says that His desire is that no one go to hell. His command is to go into the world and tell the good news of the Gospel. That is our reason for being here. There is no other! Jesus said that when everyone has heard the Gospel at least once, He will come back for us (Mark 13:10). The more faithful we are in our mission, the sooner we can leave this troubled world. I want to continue to keep this focus. There is so much noise, voices, and things to distract us from the all important job that God has given us. Let us draw courage from the saints and warriors who have blazed a path before us. Jesus said, at the age of 12, when his parents found him in the temple, "Did you not know that I must be about my Father's business?" (Luke 2:40). Jesus does only the will of his Father, which is what we are to do as well. I am recharged again as I meditate on these words. I hope you are too. God loves you immensely and is seeking an intimate relationship with you. My desire is that as you reach out to Him, His strength will infuse you with power. He gives courage to the faint. You are never alone in whatever you are facing in this life. Remember that this world is not our home; we are just passing through. Make each day count. Do something that will have eternal value.

Dad's Birthday Celebration

On January 5, 2013, our family had a birthday party for Dad at the nursing home. He was really good that night. It was a great pleasure to see him enjoy eating cake, ice cream, and other food he likes. He turned 90 years old. We took lots of pictures and cherished the memory knowing it could very well be his last birthday here on earth. While it is sad to think of losing him, it is also wonderful at the same time. I know he will be so happy in heaven to see my mother again. Since her death on December 10, 2012, we as a family are struggling to give my dad a reason to continue living. He lived to see her almost every day. It is a big adjustment for him and us as well.

31

A Scary Time with Dad
(January 31, 2013)

This is the second time my dad has done this in the last two months. He went to sleep the first time for almost three days without eating or drinking. This most recent time, we all thought he was going to die and not come out of it. I had already told my daughters that this may be the end. Then, on the fourth day, Dad woke up suddenly around 2 p.m. I went to visit him dreading what I might see. He was in his chair asleep. I touched his hand saying, "Hi Dad, it's Ruth." I did not really expect a response. What I got from him shocked me. His eyes flew wide open and he said, "Hello my dear daughter Ruth." After my initial surprise, he said that he was hungry and thirsty. I spent the next three hours giving him Sprite, orange juice, water, a bologna and cheese sandwich, pretzels, candy. It was crazy! Then he told me to go get him an order of French fries with plenty of salt and flavor on them. I called my brother who was on the way in to stop and get some. Wow! He was talking nonstop about what he had experienced the last three days while asleep. He said he was so scared and cried out to God.

I did not understand it all, but it was very interesting. He is back for now. Who knows how long? What a roller coaster ride he takes us on! The nurses at the home do not know what puts him to sleep or what wakes him up. A good possibility could be a mini-stroke. He has had several of those. We just don't know. The understanding I do have is how it is affecting me. I am anxious and on edge. I spent three days grieving and trying to prepare for the end. The emotional swings are hard to negotiate. I want to yell at my dad to stop it. However, I know he cannot help it and does not have control. I do not believe he is capable of understanding what I may be going through. Of course, I truly do not expect him to, when I am thinking clearly. Walking with him like this in his last days tends to feel like walking through a dense fog. I am blindly groping for some sense of stability. In reality I know there will be none. It will only get more rough and rocky as time goes on.

32

One Step Closer

How do you walk a mile? The answer is one step at a time. The process, for two miles or five miles, is the same. Just continue to take one more step toward the goal line, whatever that may be for you. When I heard my dad call me "his dear daughter Ruth," it felt like one giant step forward on my healing journey. Something touched me deep in my wounded soul. The tears wanted to flow, but I bit my tongue. Later at home I gave full expression to my feelings. I cried as I had not in a long time. There were tears of pain and tears of joy. I think for the first time in my life I felt loved by my father in a healthy way. It was exhilarating! The pain mixed in was that of it taking so long. I am 61 years old. I so desperately needed this as a little girl. Indeed, I did feel in a time warp. Little Ruthie soaked it up! The adult part of me was very sad because of all that I had suffered at his hands. In spite of it all, I felt healing well up from a very deep place. It was a dry place that still longed for my father's love. It is a place that no one else can fill. I have tried with three husbands. I know that I need to be aware, when and if I date in the future, that no one will take the place of my dad. That expectation leads only to an unhealthy relationship. A husband is never meant to be a father figure, but I believe that is what I tried to make them. It was an unconscious drive that I was unaware of.

The huge void is a special place that only my father's love will fill. The more healing that comes to me from the original source of pain, the less I will be drawn to abusive men or unemotionally available men—those who do not connect on a feeling level or for whatever reason are incapable of loving me. I am learning some very life-affirming lessons right now from my 90-year-old father. I am blessed. Not everyone has the opportunity to heal in this way. I had no idea how this one expression from him would make me feel. I hope that there are many more chances for me to have healing encounters with my father. He is in the early stages of dementia, so time may be short. While he still knows me, I want to visit him as often as I can. I am making this my total focus right now. As hard as it is for me to be alone, the decision not to date is a necessary and healthy choice at this time in my life. When my father has gone on to heaven, there will be a time when God will give me the desires of my heart.

I believe, as I continue to do the hard work of healing, someday there will be a companion for me. If not, I will be content in what God has called me to do and be. I pray His will be done in me. This is the cry of my heart!

33

The Roller-Coaster Ride Suddenly Ends

March 24, 2013, is the day God called my dad home to be with him. This time it was sudden and unexpected. I was in a daze, unable to believe that he could get sick one day and seven days later be gone from us. Of course, he had a connection to God, Mom, and his prayers through the years. He was social, fun-loving, loved to eat, travel in the van to church, visit friends and relatives. He always expressed how the quality of life was so important to him. When he could no longer enjoy this life, he wanted to go right to the next. That is exactly what happened. God knew his heart and honored it. He never wanted to linger as an invalid or be bedridden. He got aspiration pneumonia. We took him to the hospital immediately. He spent five days there with the antibiotics doing nothing. In fact, he got worse. Three doctors gave him no hope of recovery at 90 years old. We as a family did not want him to pass away in the hospital, so we brought him home and gathered around his bedside and sang. That was Friday evening, March 22. We cried and prayed for his comfort and ours. Sunday afternoon he was carried away by the angels to his final home. The following is a tribute that I wrote about my dad that was read at his funeral.

Tribute to Henry Redcay
My Dad

Dad trusted God with his life. He often said, "My breath is in His hands." He knew God and looked forward to spending eternity with Him. He lived in the present one day at a time and enjoyed every minute. Dad was a very positive person and was not prone to worry about the future. Dad had a grateful, thankful attitude toward God for the life he was given, even when sick. His usual parting to all was a handshake and a hearty "God bless you."

He loved to share about milking the cows and farming. He took joy in his huge garden and being able to supply plenty of fresh vegetables to feed his large family. We worked hard and Dad made sure we never went hungry. His saying was, "Take as much food as you want and eat all that you take." He hated wasting food. Dad loved to eat and enjoyed it right up until God called him home. I am sure he is now feasting at the banquet table in heaven with Jesus.

Dad brought joy and humor to all he met. He did not have to know you to start a conversation and offer a ready smile. To Dad no one was a stranger, just a friend you haven't met yet!

My daughter Angie and I were visiting Dad over the Christmas holiday this year. In his room he had the radio and the TV on. Angie said, "Grandpa, how can you listen to the radio *and* the TV both at the same time?" My dad said, "Angie, that is why God gave you two ears, one for the radio and one for the TV. Angie, didn't you know that? You must have gone to the wrong school." Angie said, "Yes, Grandpa, I guess I did." We all laughed so hard. This is just one example of my dad's sense of humor.

Dad knew God and the power of His forgiveness. He accepted responsibility for his sins, faults, and failures and asked for forgiveness. He expressed openly and freely many times through the years to me and others the great gift of forgiveness extended to him by God and his family. He experienced God's grace, forgiveness, and love.

Dad had no unfinished business left on this earth. He fought a good fight, kept the faith, and finished well. He was ready to go home when God called him. I am sure he heard the words, "Well done, good and faithful servant. Enter into the rewards that have been prepared for you from the beginning of time" (Matthew 25:23). I also want to hear those loving words from God when I take my last breath on this earth!

Part Two

34

The Braiding of Pain and Joy

I had taken a year and a half off from dating to heal and regroup from my painful divorce of 2009. I met Tim online on March 16, 2013. He wrote to me first from our "match" on E-Harmony.

I hesitated at first because he lived in Virginia. I had decided that I did not want a long-distance relationship. He continued to write and stay in contact. Then my father got sick for the last time, and passed away on March 24, leaving me very heartbroken. I wrote to Tim and told him my dad died. He was filled with empathy and prayers for me. He understood my pain and loss. This is when he really got my attention, and I wanted to get to know him better. He was able to connect with me emotionally and spiritually, which I know is my greatest need because of my past abuse. I prayed about it and felt God was leading and wanted me to open up my heart to this man.

There were things that I had learned and conditions I had set for myself in any future dating that would be critical if I were to venture into this relationship. For instance, I've learned that sexual intimacy clouds a person's objectivity. I believe with all my heart that God wishes us to wait until marriage.

Tim led the way and I responded. It felt natural and right. We exchanged phone numbers. I started to feel very bonded and close to him. I was feeling a little nervous also as this was new to me. I also knew and had shared in earlier chapters that I had past issues with feeling incomplete without a man in my life. I wanted to ensure I was not falling back into that trap.

Additionally, most men I had known in the past could not get to my heart the way Tim did. We began talking on the phone and continued to get closer to one another. We set a date to meet in person the first weekend in May. We decided I would go to his house first because I had a roommate. The trip was 123 miles, which was about a two-and-a-half-hour drive.

By the end of April, well before I was to travel to meet him, I was in love! I was so excited to meet this amazing man that God had given to me. I thought he felt the same way, but I was still nervous and not totally sure. I left home on Friday afternoon and arrived at his home around 3:30 p.m. We flew into each other's arms! It was a magical moment!

We went on to have the most wonderful weekend, better than I could ever have imagined. We ate, hiked, played ping pong, and laughed together. Tim also took me shopping and bought me a beautiful pair of earrings. Sunday morning was very special. Tim opened the car door for me in the church parking lot. We walked toward the church holding hands. Once inside, someone asked us if we were newlyweds. We were totally taken off-guard. Tim and I both looked at each other and laughed. I asked her why she thought we were newly married. She replied that it was because she saw Tim open the car door for me. Later, Tim confessed, this was the exact minute when he knew that he was in love. He told me he loved me later that same Sunday afternoon at his home. Of course, I felt I was madly in love with him also! We hugged and celebrated with a kiss on the cheek. It was the most exhilarating experience of my life!

I had prayed and asked God for a man like this for 28 long years. God really does answer prayer! I knew in 1987 that God had promised me a man like Tim. God spoke to me, promising a mate, but that it would be at his appointed time and not mine. He said, "Wait for it because it will not be behind a single day! It will surely come to pass!"

What a majestic God we serve that knows us better than we do! "He does exceedingly, abundantly above all that I could ask or think" (Ephesians

3:20). He loves to give good gifts to his children. Tim is a gift from God and I will always treasure him. I do not want to ever take him for granted or get lazy with love. It is a gift that is priceless and not to be taken lightly. God gave me the desires of my heart in his wisdom and timing.

Before I left his home Sunday for my return drive to my house, Tim and I prayed together for a safe journey home for me Sunday evening. We also prayed for God's wisdom and direction as we moved forward in our relationship. We want his will to be done in our lives for his glory. I arrived home around 8 p.m. exhausted but filled with the joy of newfound love. I can't wait to see how God is going to use us as we put Him first in our lives. We will commit to worship Him, the author and finisher of our faith. I want to hear, and I know Tim does also, the words, "Well done good and faithful servant. Enter into the joys that I have prepared for you from the beginning of time" (Matthew 25.23). God is good all the time. All the time God is good.

35
Love Deepens
(May 27, 2013)

Tim and I continue to grow in our love for each other and God. I am amazed at how God has brought us together in his perfect timing. I would not have been ready any sooner for this man of God, even though many times I thought so and was impatient. Waiting on God and following Him is so important. He knows best! Many times in His word Jesus says not to lean on our own understanding but His. We walk by faith and not by sight. How hard that is to do sometimes, but so rewarding when I am obedient to God. I see His mighty hand do things above and beyond what I could imagine. He truly does do "exceedingly, abundantly above all that I can ask or think" (Ephesians 3:20). God will always bring good out of every bad work of the enemy if we will only turn to Him and let Him. God looks to see where He can show Himself strong in our behalf. He promises to restore the years that the locust have eaten. Many years of hard work, prayers, and tears have gone into my recovery from abuse. None of it has been in vain. I want to share here the verse that I have hung onto for 28 years. This was God's promise to me in 1987 when I cried out to him for a Godly man to walk by my side for his honor and glory! It is found in Habakkuk 2:3. "For the revelation waits an appointed time; it speaks of the end and will not prove false. Though it linger, wait for it. It will certainly come and will not delay."

Wow! With Tim's love I am seeing the fulfillment of this long awaited promise. I confess that I have not always waited patiently or trusted God the way He or I wanted. I can say I did believe His promise and never gave up on His word to me. Together Tim and I want God's will done in our lives whatever that may be. We will continue to pray together and see where He leads and how He wants to use us to encourage others. I tell my story for God's glory only. Although I would prefer to be private, God's will is above what I may want. I am often selfish and need to depend on Jesus for my strength and direction. The greatest compliment anyone can give me is that they see Jesus reflected in me. Tim told me that this weekend when we were together. That brought tears to my eyes because that is the core of my heart's desire. Tim and I talk a lot about the adventure of a future together. We believe that God gave us each other as a precious gift to be treasured and never taken for granted. The covenant of marriage is God's plan and to be held in high esteem. Jesus said two are better than one because we can help each other. When one falls down, there is someone to pick us up. His plan is for man and wife to walk together in unity and to be an example of Christ and the church. We are the bride of Christ. I want to always honor and encourage my husband as the man of God that he is. What a joy it is to serve one another in love. Love is our highest calling and always will be. My desire is to pray for love to be continually evident in my life. What a wonderful promise that God looks at our hearts and not at outward appearances as the world does.

I am sure that I have only touched the surface of my understanding of God's will for me. I will grow more and more in my knowledge of Him as I make a deeper commitment to spend time in His word and prayer. I know that God loves me more than I will ever be able to fathom. It will be fully experienced only when we spend eternity with Him someday. In the meantime, He has great plans for you and me. He does miracles and makes a way when there seems to be no way. I have had many wilderness years and also many miracles in my life. I know there will be both for you, too, if you but die to self and put God first. Never forget that God is faithful and will never leave you or forsake you. That is His promise to all of us who know Him.

36

Loving God's Way
(June 18, 2013)
Another Miracle!

My relationship with Tim is very solid. We are growing in love more and more as we spend time together. Our meeting felt special from the very beginning. We both felt like this is the one. It cannot be explained; it is just like you either know it or you don't. There were conflicting things in my past with men for sure. I saw concerns, red flags, things we could not talk about. With Tim it is totally different and easy. I have never experienced anything like this before. I believe this is more normal and the way it should be in a healthy relationship. There should be no need for all kinds of drama and conflict. Real love does not hurt but helps each other grow and learn. I am sure we will have disagreements but we can discuss them and work it out. We already have talked about some tough stuff and got closer because of it. I feel totally sure and no doubt with Tim that God has put us together for His purposes. With my other three marriages, I was always conflicted about something well in advance and ignored those feelings. With Tim I have absolute peace and confidence that only God can give. I feel it in the deep well of my soul. It is a place where no one else can access but the Holy Spirit Who lives in me.

As I get to know Tim, as a mighty man of God, I grow closer to God himself. I have had a desire for an example of Jesus modeled in a man for many years. I just was not prepared for how our mutual love for each other would bond me like Super Glue to Jesus. It has created a hunger and thirst for God. A deep cleansing is taking place. The cobwebs are being swept clean. I can hear God's voice. I feel His tangible presence beside me. When I am with Tim, I feel Jesus in his hug. The love of God is in his smile. Only God knew who I needed. Through our relationship, I believe the final, deepest healing is taking place in my life. I never dreamed of this river flowing forcefully where restoration abounds.

The total expression of our love waits until marriage. We have a strong bond and commitment to do it God's way. Words are inadequate to express the joy this brings to me. Little did I envision that this decision "to wait" would produce in me feelings that in the natural world are impossible to experience? It is a deep knowing and a feeling of being pure and innocent. I feel immersed, bathed in soothing warmth, light, and love. Yes! It is a feeling of being a virgin. What an unexplainable gift for the first time in my life at 62 years of age. My past gone, just as if it never happened! This brings tears and takes my breath away. This miracle was not anywhere at all on my small radar screen. Ephesians 3:20 says that God is able "to do exceedingly, abundantly above all that I could ask or think according to the power that works in us." This is the power of God working in me for His glory.

Tim is a part of something bigger than even just us. God is using him in a majestic plan to draw others to God. We pray together every day for God's will to be done in our lives. Never have I had anything close to what this feels like. Just totally awesome! A true miracle for me! I never want to take for granted this greatest gift of love. It is a journey of trust and faith in God to show us the way. I know that we have a faithful God Who loves us more than we will ever know. He wants to give good gifts to His children just as we do with our children. Matthew 7:11 says, "If you, then, though you are evil, know how to give good gifts to your children, how much more will your Father in heaven give good gifts to those who ask him!" This life is wonderful to love and be loved. The greatest gift we have, however, is eternal life. That is God's ultimate gift and expression of His love for us. Jesus gave His life on the cross and paid the price. All you need to do is reach out and receive the gift He offers. Salvation is freely given to all who ask. I have no greater joy in life than to know God and the power of His love to draw me to Him. A deep intimate relationship with God is essential. It is the bedrock for intimacy within a marriage. God's infusion of his powerful real love and healing is preparing me for a relationship that is beyond my understanding. It is a marriage that will draw on the supernatural love of God to thrive and minister to others as well.

37

Tim's Bird's-Eye View
(June 25, 2013)

Wow! God is good! It is hard to believe that Ruth could have gone through what she went through. When I first met her, I saw a person who was full of joy, happiness, peace, and contentment. There was no evidence at all of any anger or bitterness. No sign that she had suffered such horrible abuse. She had this beautiful smile and wonderful laugh. What a miracle!

One of the first things that struck me about Ruth was her love for her dad. I could tell from the way she talked about him how deep her love was for her dad. This made it even harder for me to believe what had happened and the incredible healing in her life.

When I first learned what had happened to her, I was filled with grief and sadness. To know that someone I love so deeply suffered such horrible pain—I was full of sorrow. But it did not last long, because I know who she is now. That she has recovered, and is free of any bitterness from the past. She is free of the pain that was afflicted on her.

Hers is a story of hope. This is a remarkable good news story! For anyone who has been a victim of any kind of abuse, Ruth's story is proof that there is hope. Full recovery is possible and you can live a life of joy.

It is hard, no doubt about it. Ruth took the tough steps. She went through what was needed for healing and recovery. The fact that she did not take the easy way out is a tribute to her and an inspiration to all of us.

In the movie *Fireproof,* toward the end, Kathryn says to Caleb, "I want what you have." That is what I said to Ruth. I want what you have. She has such a close relationship with the Lord. I want that. She is at a higher level than I am. Ruth is an inspiration to me. "Whoever claims to live in Him must walk as Jesus did" (1 John 2:6). Ruth does that. Her life helps me in my walk with the Lord.

38

Meeting Tim's Extended Family
(July 29, 2013)

I was somewhat nervous as I cruised through the beautiful countryside toward Delaware. I passed luscious green meadows with grazing cows. Along the route, it was not uncommon to see a flock of wild geese in farm ponds and small streams. There were wooded hills with trees reaching toward the cloudless blue sky. I was meeting Tim this weekend at his daughter's house. She had two girls aged five and two. Questions and concerns floated to the surface and into my thoughts. What if she doesn't want to share her dad? She might feel like I am her worst nightmare of the wicked stepmother. My love for Tim could be destroyed by this woman. I felt a bit powerless facing the unknown. The following day we were also meeting his mother and sister. I was somewhat overwhelmed and yet excited about the possibility that they might like me and this could be positive. Then I prayed and let God calm my heart and mind. My Jesus had a hand in Tim and me coming together, and I knew He was in control. I could let go, and the outcome was not up to me. Tim and I prayed and believed for God's will to be done. I began to relax and picture us having a good time.

I got there before he did. He had about two hours' drive and I only one. I am an early bird, so of course I was 20 minutes ahead of him. I called him. The choice was mine to wait for him, or go in and meet her and the grandchildren. I parked a little distance away and waited. I did not want to go in without him—my security blanket. Then, after 10 minutes or so, I saw the kids look out the window and wave. That was it. I was spotted so I took a deep breath and rang the doorbell.

His daughter opened the door, smiled, and I walked in. She led me to the kitchen table and we sat down. We sat in silence for about five minutes. Then we began with some small talk. I was beginning to relax a little. Then I started sharing how hard it has been for me this year losing both my parents within three months of each other. Also I talked about the pain of my girls losing their father when they were young. Now I felt like we were connecting. She asked me what he died of at only 47 years old. The ice was broken as I shared the details with her. A few minutes later, Tim arrived. He found us in the kitchen and asked if we had been introduced to each other. She replied, "No I am just sitting here talking with someone that I have no idea who she is." I chuckled to myself thinking this is a great icebreaker. Tim and I laughed. I began to totally relax and look forward to our time together.

Things moved fast after that. We were celebrating her birthday that day. The presents were brought in and opened. She thanked us for the wonderful gifts. As a continued birthday gift, Tim and I took the kids for the day so she could have some peace and quiet. That is not exactly how we had planned the day, but I went with the flow when Tim asked me if it was okay for us to take the kids. Previously we had all planned to go to the Delaware fair together. The diaper bag was packed with milk, snacks, and extra clothes. Then we were out the door with both girls in tow along with carrying as many dolls and toys as we could. Also a DVD player came along for the half-hour ride to the children's museum.

For the next three or four hours, it became a full-time job for both of us to keep the kids safe and not lose track of them. In the end we had lots of fun but were so exhausted. We went home to rest for about a half hour before dinner. I wish I could say that dinner went well but not so. It was quite the challenge and topped our list of things never to do again with just the two of us. At Tim's suggestion, we went to Hibachi Grill where he thought it would be easy buffet-style. Great idea, we expressed to each other. No waiting for our food and restless kids. In reality what happened was rice and noodles all over the floor.

We had an unhappy waitress coming to sweep up the mess every time we left the table.

Tim and I were hungry and tired. The children were just plain tired and restless. They could not sit still long enough for us to eat, much less enjoy it. I was so relieved when it was over. On the way home, we were able to laugh about it and express the common phrase of live and learn. His daughter and husband were out for dinner alone in peace and quiet. I sure was ready for some of that myself!

Now it was time to move on to Sunday, which was a total hoot in a good way. Tim and I took the girls to church with us. They did so well and we were able to enjoy the service. The party started after church when we picked up his daughter and her husband for lunch. The destination was an Italian restaurant to meet Tim's mother and sister. I can truly say that this was pure fun. There is nothing like the laughter of Italian families with food. His sister brought pictures of her son's recent wedding to share with me, along with periodic shouts for everyone to eat, eat, and eat. I soon learned that with Italians, sharing food creates an atmosphere of love and laughter. We did laugh heartily and eat, but we could not eat all of the food in spite of our best intentions. Not to worry—it was boxed up and taken home to eat later. Wasting good food was not acceptable! I do agree with this. My family rule was the same.

When we got home, the youngest one got a bath and went to bed. The last hour after that, Tim and I went downstairs and played on the floor with the five-year-old grandchild. It was very peaceful and quiet. I was amazed at the fun I had dressing the Barbie dolls and finding shoes and accessories to match the outfits. I also got Barbie's husband Ken ready for a swimming party and boat ride. It is continued healing for me to be with children. Their innocence and imagination gives me the insight into a childhood that I never had. It was also a great sharing and bonding time with Tim and his granddaughter. I feel so blessed to be part of a loving family! God is so good in restoring back to me what had been taken. He promised to do that, and His word is true.

I got back home to Pennsylvania around 8 p.m., dead tired but very happy with great memories of our weekend together with Tim's extended family.

39

A Weekend Together at the Beach

On a cloudy Friday morning, July 9, 2013, Tim and I drove toward Wildwood beach. We were excited to be spending our first vacation weekend together at the Jersey Shore. Along for the ride were preparations in case of rain. The obvious, of course, was an umbrella and a game of checkers. The forecast was not looking good. We said as we drove that we did not want the weather to ruin our time together. Our intent was to have a good time no matter what. The check-in time at our motel was 3 p.m. To our surprise, when we arrived at 12:30, it was ready for us. We walked to a restaurant nearby and had lunch. Around 1:30, as we headed for a spot on the beach, the sun came out. Tim and I looked at each other and smiled. No words were needed. I was thankful for the sun. Even more than that, however, rising to the surface was something more important. It was a feeling of deepening love for this wonderful man by my side. I became aware of such thankfulness for this blessing in my life. Only God could have brought us together at exactly the right time. Also my thoughts included the miracle of God's love in me. Without that, it would be impossible to love Tim after all the horror that I had experienced in the past at the hands of abusive men. My blessings increased as we spread out our towels on the beach. I expressed my feelings to Tim. His response validated that the feelings I had for him were mutual. He was aware of how deep and intimate our love had become. Our desire exploded in a prayer of rejoicing in Him. We prayed together that we would always strive to listen and obey God's voice. Our highest aim was to please Him Who loves us beyond our wildest dreams.

Around 5 p.m. a sudden storm came up and drove us and most of the others off the beach in a rush. We were safely in our motel when the sky opened up and dumped buckets of water over the beach town of Wildwood, New Jersey. It did not last long but left huge ponds of water everywhere. We thought it was over and headed for the boardwalk. We did take the umbrella just in case. It was a good decision because it did rain again for a short time. Then the sun came out while it was still raining. Then the most beautiful rainbow appeared over the boardwalk as the rain stopped. Tim and I, along with the crowd, could only stand in awe of this spectacular sight. Every time I see such beauty, I feel close to God and his promises. He said He would put a rainbow in the sky as His promise to us that He will never again destroy the world in a flood as He did in the days of Noah. How great and mighty is our God! We worshiped Him in our hearts. What a treat for us on our first vacation together!

We went on to enjoy the evening as well as the rest of our weekend with no rain. It was perfect beach weather. The ocean water was a warm 73 degrees. It sure felt a whole lot colder than that at first, but once we were in it for a while, it was delightful. We laughed a lot and ate junk food. I threw out my diet for the vice of whatever I wanted, for this short time. My favorite foods at the shore are pizza, fries, and ice cream. We also rode on the giant Ferris wheel. It was such a fantastic view from the top.

On the way home Sunday afternoon, we stopped at Stone Harbor beach to visit Tim's Uncle Frank. He is 93 years old and a World War II veteran. Uncle Frank was one of the funniest men I had met in a long time. He lived with his daughter Pauline and her husband EJ. They teased Frank and rolled their eyes. We ended up staying a whole lot longer than planned, but I did not mind at all. What a good memory of him and his family from this visit. I felt really in awe and blessed yet again at the wonder of God's human creation.

I got home about 9 p.m. Sunday evening really tired but very content and happy. What good memories Tim and I will always cherish for the rest of our days together. God is good all the time. All the time God is good! Tim and I had amazing joy in our hearts. We kept God first and foremost in our sights. We honored and obeyed Him. What a blessing God has in store for us in our marriage. We have an unshakeable foundation built on the rock that never moves or changes. My hope is built on nothing less than Jesus' blood and righteousness.

40

The Ring
(July 18, 2013)

Tim and I were excited! Today was the day we were ready to go shopping. It was not just ordinary stuff we were looking for. Tim wanted to make sure that I found the perfect engagement ring. Once inside the mall it became overwhelming. There were four top-notch jewelry stores to choose from. In the first store I found a special ring that quickly became my favorite. We decided, however, to take our time and check out all four stores. After looking in all four, we were exhausted. We went home to sleep on it. This was an important decision. I lay in bed that night unable to sleep. I thought about the one ring I saw in the first store we were in. I began to feel sad thinking that someone else may have bought it and I would never see it again. That was the beginning of realizing I had found my dream ring. Somehow it had already attached itself to my finger and would not let go.

In the morning, I told Tim about it. After church, we again headed for the store where my ring was waiting for me. I began to worry about what I would do if it was no longer there. I calmed myself by thinking it was the very next day after spotting it. What are the chances out of all those hundreds of rings that someone bought this one?

Wow, I was floating on cloud 9, or maybe 10, when I discovered it was still there. It looked even more beautiful than the night before. I turned to Tim. This is the one I want! That was all it took. He bought it right then and there. It was sterling silver with a braided look to it. Two diamonds were on either side of a larger diamond in the middle. The ring with its three diamonds reminded me of my faith in the Trinity as well as the union of husband and wife enjoined with the presence of God. The ring felt alive and I believe that was also what enthralled me with it so much. It was sent out for sizing, which would take about two weeks. The plan was that, when it was finished, Tim would take possession of it and decide how and when to make a formal proposal. It was all happening so fast. In my heart and soul, though, I knew Tim was whom God had chosen for me. He was totally different from my ex-husbands. I prayed and thanked God for the wonderful gift He had given me. I went to sleep that night with great peace in my heart and a smile on my face.

Tim and I got married on June 21, 2014. What a wonderful day it was as we shared our love and vows with each other! After our wedding we went on a week-long honeymoon in the Chesapeake Bay area. We were so blessed with every day being sunny, warm and beautiful. God gave us some of the most spectacular sunsets we have ever seen. It felt like they were just for us with his smile and enjoyment of our marriage also.

Part Three

41

Three Years Later!
(October 4, 2017)

Blindsided and Duped!

My therapist. She is a Godly, compassionate, soft-spoken woman. "How do you feel about writing a letter to Tim?" she said in almost a whisper. I knew I could not do it yet. Just the thought of talking to him, even on paper that I did not intend to send, made me feel sick in my stomach. I did have lots of random words, however, running around in my mind. "Well, go ahead and write those down," she responded back to me. So I went home and this is what I wrote:

The ultimate betrayal, anger, rage, revenge, hate, mean, cruel, evil, lies, unbelievable, denial, cannot be happening, unfair, shame, depressed, alone, fear, grief, pain, tears, sorrow, sadness, stunned, paralyzed, abandoned, frozen, heartbroken, broken promises, loss, why, raw open wound, death of the dream, final, over, gone. I feel lost in a maze of emotions, where every direction feels like a dead-end street. I feel so alone in my search for an answer!

My husband Tim has filed for divorce, and on October 6 it became final. We were married for only three years. Wow! To go through and talk about yet a fourth divorce is unthinkable, unbelievable! Yet that is the reality of what happened. There was no real reason to speak of, other than he decided he did not want to do the work that a good marriage takes.

Some of the work he refused to face was his hateful only daughter and son-in-law. I could write another whole book on just this drama. If I were writing for a TV soap opera, this would top them all. But really, what good would it do and how would it be helpful to you, my friends and readers? I just want to share my opinion and agree with God's word here. The Bible says in 1 Timothy 6:10: "For the love of money is the root of all kinds of evil. Some people, eager for money, have wandered from the faith and pierced themselves with many griefs!" I believe greed and lust for money from his daughter had a lot to do with the destruction of our marriage.

Tim let all kinds of evil happen, and believe me, I have never seen anything like it and never want to again! Tim hardened his heart against God and me. He changed into a stranger right before my eyes. I no longer recognized the man I had known and fallen in love with. All the promises that he had made to me, that divorce was not an option, went right out the window along with his love!

Jesus said that because of the hardness of men's hearts divorce occurs. I have experienced this man to be the cruelest person I have ever met to date, because we had talked so much about my hurts of childhood abuse and also three prior marriages and divorces. I made it clear to him that another divorce in out of the question. If you are not that person or are not sure, then walk away! But he continued to reassure me that divorce would not be an option. So you can only imagine how horrible this betrayal is for me, and the healing journey ahead is huge! He even did an edit on this book and knew all the details of my hurt.

I know God had a way through for us, but you have to want it and he did not. I made mistakes, of course, because I am only human. When in extreme pain and trauma, it is easy to lash out in anger. However, I loved him until the end and did all I could to save our marriage. The bottom line is that in the end he will answer to God and not me! We all will give account someday to God. He gives us free will and sometimes people make decisions against His will. It takes two committed people to make a marriage work and only one to break that commitment and it is done.

Commitment has to be the foundation of any marriage or successful relationship.

Just because someone isn't willing or able to love us, it doesn't mean that we are unlovable!

42

Pain and Grief!
(October 27, 2017)

Once again I am fighting for my life! I cry for hours until the exhaustion takes over and I stare off into the blackness. I feel like this will be the final straw that takes me down. I cannot sleep. I beg God to get Tim to change his mind and Love me. I eat but taste nothing. I feel so much anger!

The why questions torment my mind constantly. Why didn't God warn me about him when we were dating that he was a predator. Why didn't He protect me from this agony when I had already gone through so much pain in my life? I did not deserve this! I force myself to keep breathing. Somehow even this becomes hard to do and saps my energy. I go on long walks to stay sane. I beat the trees with sticks until the sweat pours off my face and into my eyes. My knees buckle in pain as I collapse in a pitiful heap. All I know is that somehow the knife in my heart is relentless.

I am terrified by the fierceness of my anger. Later I learned that the energy of anger helped keep me alive and away from hopeless depression, which came eventually. This is normal in the grief process. It was many, many months of panic, fear, and dread. The hole just felt too deep this time. I had doubts of whether I could make it through.

Thoughts of suicide danced in my head. The one and only bright thought that kept me fighting was my two beautiful daughters. I was so loved by them! They lost their father some 19 years ago. All they have as a parent is me. I could not bear to die and hurt them for the rest of their lives. I just could not be that selfish. I had to find a way to go on no matter what I faced.

My wonderful therapist was an angel who helped me to stay afloat somehow. The challenges I faced were so numerous that at times I just wanted to go to the hospital and sleep. I would dream that when I woke up, it would just be a nightmare and not real. Denial still wanted to be my friend. But I could not stay with denial. I had to accept the reality of this major life change. There was also the strong feelings of wanting to let myself get bitter and hard. Then I could never get hurt again. It was easy when in that much pain to view Love as the enemy. I fought hard against that happening. I knew it would take a long time, but I had no choice but to eventually forgive Tim and let it go. Oh! But how impossible those thoughts are when your heart is crushed and your spirit is dried up inside of you. Forgiveness is in my experience a supernatural act.

They say that healing takes time. I believe that. The problem is that time stands still and refuses to move. Slow and agonizing, the ticking of the clock is very annoying to me. Each day at night is the worst. The lost pieces of my heart are felt as raw pain. It is about two weeks now since that truck came and I loaded up all my stuff and I said good-bye to what I believed was my life forever with my husband.

He had said, "until death do us part." Death would have been easier than lies, betrayal, rejection, abuse, and being devalued as a woman, a person. This was on purpose! An accidental death I would have grieved so much differently and with compassion. Now anger bangs on my door for attention. Where is justice for the cruel behaviors of one who had claimed to Love me? With my tear-stained face and red eyes, I somehow choose to let myself hope a little.

I have been in so much deep pain that each breath was sheer torture. Total exhaustion came over my soul and mind. The dreadful darkness was oppressive. It seemed to smother me and felt like a nightmare in my heart. My trusting, open, loving heart was cruelly mistreated and ripped from my chest! Do you have an understanding of the horror of this kind of pain? Have you experienced a terrible sorrow that seems difficult to reconcile with God's perfect Love? A sorrow that comes crashing down on you. A sea of storms without one bit of hope. I am sure that many of you, my readers, can identify with pain and loss of some kind. If not yet, it will most likely touch you before life is over. Human life is a maze of brightness, gloom, shadows, dark clouds, tears and sunshine! The only hope I see is to continue coming back to the cross. The dreadful darkness of Calvary and the feeling of Jesus having been forsaken on the cross for you and me. He is ready to accompany us through the valley of the shadow of death. Yes, even the death of my fourth marriage, which in my mind I would not survive. Indeed I did come close to finally just letting go and going insane. The cumulative effect of all my losses was just too much!

43

Depression and Looking Back!

Finally the anger stage began to subside. I was so relieved to have that raw rage and the debilitating hurt somewhat behind me. What I did not realize at the time was how much energy the anger and pain was giving to me and helping me survive. When I began to notice that I was depressed, it was very frightening. I felt so tired, totally washed out and drained spiritually, emotionally and physically. Depression was a more silent, insidious killer. It reeked of hopelessness, despair, and wanting to just quit the fight for life and health. I did know that this was serious and had great potential to take me all the way down. I felt so vulnerable and lonely! Fear also wanted to enter in to help depression along. I was aware of the severe danger and decided to fight this war whatever it took.

It would take my wholehearted decision and lots of hard work to climb out of the battle against depression. My wonderful therapists suggested that I go to the doctor and get some anti-depression medication to help take the edge off and battle more successfully. She did not want me to sink too low and not be able to rise again. She knew how deceiving depression can be and how easy it is to give up. I did go to the doctor and get the medication, which gave me the temporary boost that I needed to avoid going under. I am still on it today as I write, but the depression is mild and manageable now. Someday I believe I will be able to stop taking the medication. It does not matter, though, and brings me no shame if I need to keep taking it. The medication is not a cure but a tool that helps me fight better. I still have to do the hard work every day and sometimes every hour or minutes. The main goal is to continue the journey God has me on. I have a strong will to live and never give up, no matter how hard life gets! I want to be healthy in all areas of my life. I lean heavily on God's help! Without Him I don't believe I could or would have survived this fourth divorce.

I discovered another component of my thinking that was feeding depression. I call it a merry-go-round and also a dead-end street. It goes something like this: if only I would have, I wish I could have, I should have, maybe the end result would be different if only I had not done or said such and such. You get the picture of this circular thinking that is crazy-making stuff. It is made up of regret and so hard to let go of. It is in the past and cannot be changed. The circular motion just feeds hopelessness and despair. Looking back does nothing to aid healing. I must strongly resist walking down this dead-end street called torture. Sometimes I feel so desperate to go back, but the past can never be changed no matter how much I struggle to do so. I will chose life in the present. This day today is the only one that is precious and must not be lost. God is on this path with me called life and now. At the end of this street is gold, light, eternity, and Joy. It is not easy street and never will be, but the rewards are certain. At the end of this street I meet Jesus. The smell is sweet, beautiful. I inhale deeply the peace that dwells there.

I am reminded of Lot and his wife as they were fleeing from the cities of Sodom and Gomorrah. God was destroying these cities by fire and brimstone because of their great wickedness. He instructed Lot and his wife to run, leave, and do not look back. God wanted their hearts to be on Him and His provision for them in the future. It seems to me rather harsh, but I believe there is a lesson here for me and us right now. Lot's wife disobeyed God and looked back. She was instantly turned into a pillar of salt. I want to obey God and trust His word. When I was forced out of my marriage, God was saying, "Don't look back. There is nothing there but wickedness and fire." I do not want to become frozen and immobilized like a pillar of salt. God wants to lead me to the Promised Land. I must look ahead and walk by faith and total surrender to what He has for me. In Philippians 3:13, Paul says to forget those things which are behind and press forward. It does take a lot of work and awareness to be able to let go, face the future, and focus on the present. I will make a deliberate chose to live in the present. The effort and reward is well worth it! It cannot be done apart from the supernatural connection and relationship with God through prayer, the power of the working of the Holy Spirit in our lives. In my flesh and humanness I want to go back with anger and revenge on the betrayal and wickedness of my ex-husband. However, when I listen to Jesus, He says that vengeance is His. He will repay. I need to keep myself out of it and leave him to God Who is the master of justice someday. I rest in His Word and let go! Jesus says to pray for our enemies and those who spitefully use us. It is so hard to do, but this is where the miracle of healing begins! I consider that our present sufferings are not worth comparing with the glory that will be revealed in us. Romans 8:18.

Wow, what glorious hope in God's work and promises. I could not go on without it!

I choose to hold onto hope and believe for a miracle just because God said I can!

I love what the Bible says in Romans 8: 31–37 (King James Version):

What shall we then say to these things? If God be for us, who can be against us? He that spared not his own Son, but delivered him up for us all, how shall he not with him also freely give us all things? Who shall lay anything to the charge of God's elect? It is God that Justifies. Who is he that condemneth? It is Christ that died, yea rather, that is risen again, who is even at the right hand of God, who also makes intercession for us. Who shall separate us from the love of Christ?

Now listen to this awesome answer to the question:

Shall tribulation, or distress, or persecution, or famine, or nakedness, or peril, or sword. . . . Nay! In all these things we are more
than conquerors through him that loved us.

Well, if this does not cover it all, there is more in verses 38 and 39:

For I am persuaded, that neither death, nor life, nor angels, nor prin-
cipalities, nor powers, nor things present, not things to come, nor
height, nor depth, nor any other creature, shall be able to separate
us for the love of God which is in Christ Jesus our Lord.

These words are riches beyond this world to hold onto. The best treasure
that you and I will ever have on this earth!

44

Struggles, Lessons, Healing
(February 2018)

Saying Goodbye to My Dad

Dear Dad,

I am feeling very, very angry with you for what you did to me. I was an innocent little girl. I was your daughter. I trusted you, loved you, and adored you. How could you abuse, rape, and destroy me like you did? Not just once but a decision made by you over and over again to rape me year after year. You will never know or understand how horrible and unspeakable this crime against me was. I was damaged, betrayed, and hurt in ways that will take a lifetime to heal from.

I have looked for your love and acceptance my whole life. I have wanted to know that I am lovable and worth being treated well. I have looked for you in my husbands. I have wanted them to show me and give me the unconditional love that as a child I should have gotten from you. I wanted them to make me feel lovable. I have found you yet again in my fourth husband.

I found abuse again and again. Men like you, Dad, who are not willing or able to love me. The pain, damage, and wounds run deep. I will never understand how you were so brutal and heartless. My fourth ex-husband reminds me so much of you, Dad. I try and try to get him to stop abusing me and to love me but he will not. He is sick and twisted, just like you were, Dad.

I am sixty-six years old and still looking for your love! I have forgiven you but I can never forget. I was robbed by you of so much. You have no idea how evil and wicked this sin against me was. This is taking me a lifetime to heal. I have made a decision to stop looking for you. All you have to offer me is continued pain and suffering. You were never a father of Love and never will be. I am saying good-bye to you forever!

I am looking to God, my Abba, Father. He is the only one I can fully trust. He alone will love me, restore and heal me.

I have nothing more to say. I don't want you in my life anymore! You are dead and can no longer speak into my life. If you try, I will no longer listen or acknowledge you. I am moving on with my life. Good-bye Dad forever! I bury you. You are not good for me and never will be! Your daughter, Ruth

I felt really good after I expressed myself to Dad in this letter. Then I had this wonderful experience that I share with you now!

God spoke to me about a scene I witnessed while in the ocean at Ocean City, Maryland. It was seeing a father far out in the ocean facing six- to eight-foot waves. In his arms was his four-year-old daughter. She delighted in every wave! Why? Simple answer is she was in her daddy's arms. She knew that he would keep her safe and hold her high above the huge waves. She was not afraid or in any doubt that daddy would take care of her. There was perfect love and trust in her daddy. In the midst of my intense waves coming at me I heard the voice of God saying. "Do you trust your Daddy that much? Do you trust Me to hold you and lift you high above the giant waves that are coming at you? Will you dare to trust My love and care for you as your Daddy God, the good, good Father? You can let go and rest in My arms just as that little girl did in the ocean. I have got you! No fear, only trust! Live every day resting in Daddy's arms!" I began to cry as this lesson hit home in my heart. I so longed to feel Loved and know that I can stop the pain and struggling. When God speaks and shows me how much He loves me in this example, I am strengthened to continue on. I am not alone, and He is walking with me always.

I struggle, just as I am sure many of you do. The age-old question is why? Why is there so much pain, loss, and suffering in this world? I don't understand or know all of the answer. All I can do is press into Jesus to know Him better and receive His Love when I feel like I can't stand the pain any longer! Many times I see no purpose whatsoever for the bad things that happen beyond my control. I admit to being angry at God and struggling to stay afloat. But God understands my humanness. He can hear and feel my churning emotions, tears, and sleepless nights. Even on my absolute worst days of doubting God, I believe by faith in His word that He is with me and loves me. But where else would I turn to if not Him? What else or who else is there if not God? So with this knowledge in my heart I continue to cry out to Jesus in my pain and grief.

I cannot afford to wait until understanding comes or answers to my "Why?" I need help now, urgently, to keep from drowning in my sorrows and loss! Maybe that is just a small glimmer of some meaning from our suffering. Our total dependence on a power greater than ourselves. What if God wanted me to learn that this world is not my home? I am just here for a very short time. A purpose to keep us close to Him. A reason to walk by faith and not by sight (2 Corinthians 5:10). I am so human and very needy. Trying to go through this life alone without God is not an option for me.

I hope you make the same decision for yourself! Oh, don't get me wrong. I hate not knowing why. I probably always will. However, I must go and depend on Jesus' Life and words to me. The Bible is our road map. He says that in this world we will have tribulation, but to be of good cheer because He has overcome the world (John 16:33). As Helen Keller also said, "Although this world is full of suffering, it is also full of the overcoming of it,"

He told us these things so we can have peace in our hearts when they are stomped on and broken. This helps a lot with the why: just having God tell us ahead of time what this world will be like. God really, really loves us fiercely. There is a revelation coming to me about when human beings reject us and betray us. Our value does not decrease because of someone else's inability to see our worth! My value is based on who God says that I am, and no other humans' word, especially ungodly ones'. Satan is a master at lies, and the ungodly agree with him! So sad! We are fighting in a spiritual war. We must know the truth of God's word. It is the only thing that will free us!

There will be down times and hardships when I don't feel okay. Even then I am okay because my good, good Father tells me that I am! My foundation, my rock is His promises to me! Oh, it is not that feelings are not important. They are to be felt and validated. Not stuffed or ignored. Jesus experienced all the range of emotions that we have. He cares how we are feeling! So I come to him with open hands and let go of the broken, irreversible past into God's hands. I step out into the invincible future with him. I am lovable and precious. God loves me unconditionally.

I commit to move forward beyond abuse. I commit to forgive, heal, and Love again!

45

Healing and Learning
(January 14, 2018)

I am beginning to navigate life's ups and downs a bit better now. I don't try to predict how life is going to go. There is no way that we can always prepare for our unknown circumstances. The only solid hope is to build a strong foundation that supercedes our circumstances. Hebrews 10:23 says it like this: "Let us hold unswerving to the hope we profess, for He who promised is faithful!" This is the only thing that we can count on for sure with no doubts! This life can and is full of pain, suffering, betrayal, and loss, broken promises from those we loved and trusted; unfaithfulness and lies coming at us when least expected.

Our roots must go deep into a relationship with God and His Word. Any other foundation will not be real or lasting. When the storms come, if we are depending on the foundation of this world, we will be destroyed. Our soul, mind, emotions will be broken by bitterness, unforgiveness, hate, and many other tools used by the enemy to separate us from God. We can only hold and love others to the extent that we know we are held and loved by God! This is a rich revelation from God that I have missed for so many years.

I am just now beginning to understand at a whole new level what real Love is and what it really means from God's point of view and not the ungodly world's.

46

Passion
(March 14, 2018)

If you had a cure for cancer, you would want to shout it out to everyone from the rooftops. You would want all who had it to know the cure and be healed. That is why I share Jesus with you: because He has the cure for our malignant souls. Eternity is too long to live without Him. We must impact our sphere of influence for Him! We must touch at least one person with Jesus' Love every day. His Love pierces the darkness with light. His Love drives out hate. I weep for lost souls who refuse Him. God's heart is broken when His free gift of salvation is rejected! I cry out to God that He will break my heart for what breaks his! As long as there is one human being who does not know Jesus, I feel a debt of service to that person until he does make a decision for Christ.

Our main motivation for service is Love for others, but mainly Love for our Lord and obedience to Him. If our caring is only for the cause of humanity, we will most likely encounter a great deal of ingratitude from other people that will discourage us and drag us down in despair. However, if our desire is to serve God, no amount of ingratitude will be able to hinder us from serving one another and sharing the good news. When it really gets in our soul and Spirit that Jesus served us when we were lost in the depths of meagerness, selfishness, and sin, then it enables us to let nothing we encounter from others take away our determination to serve for His sake.

Ephesians 6:10–18 (The Message):

And that about wraps it up. God is strong, and he wants you strong. So take everything the Master has set out for you, well-made weapons of the best materials. And put them to use so you will be able to stand up to everything the Devil throws your way. This is no afternoon athletic contest that we'll walk away from and forget about in a couple of hours. This is for keeps, a life-or-death fight to the finish against the Devil and all his angels. Be prepared. You are up against far more that you can handle on you own. Take all the help you can get, every weapon God has issued, so that when it's all over but the shouting, you'll still be on your feet. Truth, righteousness, peace, faith and salvation are more than words. Learn how to apply them. You'll need them throughout your life. God's Word is an indispensable weapon. In the same way, prayer is essential in this ongoing warfare. Pray hard and long. Pray for your brothers and sisters. Keep your eyes open. Keep each other's spirits up so that no one falls behind or drops out.

I will walk with purpose. One day at a time. A grateful heart is protecting me from negative thinking, which is very toxic for my soul and spirit. It will paralyze productivity, purpose, and God's plan for my life. If the enemy cannot get me to walk away from God, he will try to destroy my purpose and from fulfilling God's will for my life. As God's power enables me, I will strive to walk in gratitude, which will keep me centered in God's presence and unconditional Love! God has always taken care of me in the past. I am confident that He will continue in the present and future. I will praise and worship Him for the majestic being that He is!

As I continue to walk with God through this incredible pain, miracles happen in the midst of it all. I cannot figure out how. I see things and hear His voice whisper to my soul when the knife is twisting in my heart. I feel as if the pain will make it stop beating. But I tell it to keep going.

To date this has been the worst pain I have ever experienced. I am beginning to see amazing truths that I have never had insight into before this happened. I am starting to view my trials as great opportunities instead of large obstacles. Behold, I am starting to know God in a whole new way! Every problem comes with a promise and a provision (Luke 12:31, 32). It is a design from God to elevate me. Upgrade my thinking into how God sees me.

Two questions to ask God in every situation: "What does this mean? And what must I do?" The purpose of everything in my life is to make me more like Christ! If I see that God has chosen to show and prove His great Love to me through every difficult situation, it enables me to find a place of rest and shelter in Him. It also shows others His endless power to keep and nourish me and you. Every storm cloud turns into a beautiful rainbow. Without the storm and the rain, no rainbow is possible. So in the process every difficult situation becomes one of transformation, ascension, and glorification. The most precious jewels are often formed and delivered by very trying times and by very difficult people.

How wonderful that within the package I will find the very treasures of the King's palace and the Bridegroom's endless Love!

I choose to trust the Lord through the darkness and honor Him. I choose unwavering confidence even in the midst of my painful rejection and betrayal by my husband. The reward of my faith will be that of an eagle. I will fly high above the fear and doubt. I will receive a renewed sense of youth and strength. One day at a time; God sees beyond today and is holding me tenderly in His arms. There is safety and peace, mercy and grace in my time of need. It is always darkest before the dawn. God lights up in front of me one step at a time so that I do not stumble and fall. My walk is sure and steadfast. The Lord leads me to a place of safety; He rescues me because He delights in me! Wow! How amazing! Let's say that again: God delights in me and in you! (Psalm 18:19, New Living Translation).

47

The Enemy
(April 2018)

I have reminded myself today of who my real enemy is and what his goal and purpose is for my life. It is a direct and totally opposite force to God. The real enemy wants me distracted by people who don't like me. Decisions that loved ones may make that cause pain and emotional stress.

The real enemy does work in and through people who give him permission to do so. Open up our eyes to see the reality that our true enemy is Satan and his evil spirits and strongholds. They operate and try to derail us through people. Nothing is new since the Garden of Eden. The enemy of our souls came to Adam and Eve. The deception and goal are the same in our case as in theirs! It is to cause us to separate ourselves from God, because he knows how powerful that connection is. Satan was an angel and lived with God in heaven before he was thrown down to earth for sin and rebellion against God. He therefore hates God and all who follow Him. He wants us to believe lies about God, such as "He doesn't love you or you would not be going through pain." "He must not care or you would not have gotten cancer." "He has forsaken you because your loved one has died or deserted you."

He can only get a foothold in our lives to the extent that we believe his lies about God and His character. We need to be fully convinced that His word is absolute truth. Fiercely hungry to digest his unconditional Love for us. To trust and know by faith that His ways are the best whether we understand it or not. We walk by faith and not by sight.

Guard your heart, because out of it come the issues of life. The enemy comes to steal, kill, and destroy the word of God from our minds and hearts. In light of this truth, we do not go after people in our battle. We do not fight with flesh and blood! Ephesians 6:12 says it like this: "For we wrestle not against flesh and blood, but against the rulers of the darkness of this world, against spiritual wickedness in high places" (King James). It is so impossible to walk in this truth without the supernatural insight and control of the Holy Spirit of God himself inside of us. In my natural self I so want to see people as the enemy and go after them with my rage and hurt! I am now learning this hard but awesome lesson. My enemy has never been husband number 4, 3, 2, 1, or any other temptation that has come to me in human form. They are only vessels like me to be used for good and God's purposes or for evil and the devil's plan, schemes, and lies. We must all decide to yield ourselves to one or the other. It cannot be both. Jesus says that if we are not for Him than we are against Him.

I have decided to follow my Master God into whatever He has for me. What a giant load of relief off our souls when there is this promise of no lies and only eternal Love forever! "I will not forget you, I have written your name on the palms of my hands" (Isaiah 49: 15, 16).

The explosion of understanding and light has gone off in my heart. Don't let your mistakes define you. Don't let rejection from others define you. Don't let abuse define you. The only one that defines you and me is God's word. He defines us as precious sons and daughters of the King! We are forgiven by His blood and resurrection. The enemy's number one weapons are lies that go against God's word. That is why we must know the truth and it will set us free!

By the way, this is not a once and done deal. Over and over again, each day of our lives, will come times of testing and trials. Many times I have had to and will have to pray and work hard to resist and sort out the lies from the truth. The lies will take us down into despair, but the truth will lift us up to joy and peace. There are weapons formed against us, but God promised us that no weapon formed against us will prosper. The weapons will be different depending sometimes on our circumstances.

Right now for me the enemy wants me coated in feelings of shame. Shame is not of God, so I fight. It is a lie and has power only if I let it deceive me and believe it. It is so vital for me to say again that we have no option but to know the truth in order to win the war against us. Only who God says that I am matters and not people. Only God can be totally trusted to define me accurately. I am a child of God and precious to Him. I am lovable and deeply loved by Him! All that I need is in Him. I commit to moving forward. I commit to forgive, heal, and love again!

48

April 12, 2018

I left my lawyer's office today after a meeting with her. I felt tired and hurt all over my body and emotions. Here I am, a little over six months divorced, and a new wave of grief has washed over my soul. My ex still is as cruel as I experienced him in our marriage. I had just learned that next week I will be dragged by him into court fighting about money. I became livid again! Anger and rage caused me to lash out on the elevator wall as I rode down to the lobby and into the street.

People walking, waiting for a bus, business as usual in the city. "This should not be," I mumbled to myself. "Everything is all wrong!" I wanted to shout it among the crowds. I hated that alone feeling walking down the sidewalk to my car. Many words went through my head that I felt like saying to him. In my humanness and pain pretty normal. But of course I knew I would not stay here.

The thing is, I would understand and have compassion for him if he truly could not afford to give me any financial help. However, I happen to know that he has more than he will ever need, and this really rubs me the wrong way. He will never miss it, and I desperately need it. I don't hate him, but I do hate the greed and revengeful behavior from him. Divorce is unthinkable enough without this on top of it. If he doesn't want to be married, fine, but the very least he could do is help me get on my feet again after betrayal and rejection. Sometimes I really want to smack him hard on the side of his head to wake him up. Of course I will not, because I am committed to leave revenge to God. But Oh! How extremely difficult that is at a time like today. The love of money truly is the root of all kinds of evil, as the bible declares.

"How sad," I said to myself as I was driving home. "How can God Love people who behave like this?" Here is just one person I know, but millions live in rebellion and disobedience to God and His will and word. How could He die for sins like this? How can He love me unconditionally? I have also done hurtful things to others. I have since repented, and thankfully, He freely forgives. I will decide to pray and believe God will open up Tim's eyes to see the truth before it is too late. I will rise strong again and not let the enemy defeat me!

49

Perseverance

God's love and forgiveness can pardon and restore any and every kind of sin or wrongdoing. It doesn't matter who you are or what you have done. It doesn't matter if you have deliberately oppressed or even murdered someone, or how much you have abused yourself or others. In Luke 15, remember the story of the prodigal son? The runaway son knew that in his father's house there was abundance of food and Love. He also discovered that there was grace to spare and instant forgiveness. The key was coming home to the father. Many times we go away and need to come home again and again. The Father is always the same, running out to meet us even before we get there.

Courage is not the absence of fear, but the conquering of it. It is not how many times you fall that matters, but how many times you get up again. Read Romans 8:38 and 39. Be encouraged that nothing—and that means nothing—will be able to separate us from His Love. I don't know about you, but I sure need these promises to hang onto with the horror that I am going through with my ex-husband.

God dropped this story in my heart to share with you. It is found in Exodus 3:7–8, 10 (New International Version) where God says:

> I have indeed seen the misery of my people in Egypt. I have heard them crying out because of their slave drivers, and I am concerned about their suffering. So I have come down to rescue them from the hand of the Egyptians and to bring them up out of that land into a good and spacious land, a land flowing with milk and honey.

God wanted to use one of His servants called Moses for this job. He told him to go now because "I am sending you."

There are two truths that God is revealing to me right now through this story. Number one is that He sees, hears, and is concerned about my suffering and bondage, whatever it may be. What a great comfort this is to know about God! He is doing this with you also in your trials, whatever they are, as you cry out to Him for help and deliverance. Number two is that God will deliver us from slavery and lead us to our Promised Land flowing with milk and honey. I was picturing in my mind and tasting what milk and honey represents and why God used these two words for us. Milk is nourishing and soothing. Many say to drink warm milk before bedtime to relax and sleep better. Milk baths are recommended for a relaxing and peaceful experience. Honey I love also. Sweet and smooth. It is very healthy and, also like milk, is used for so many purposes. It is a mighty great healing agent indeed. So the land flowing with these two ingredients of milk and honey is an awesome, very exciting feeling for me. God promises to lead us there, so it is a sure thing because He always keeps His Word! I like the word "flowing," which suggest abundance and continuity. Press into Him. Hunger and thirst for this and you will be delivered! Proverbs 29:18 says, "If my people can't see what God is doing they stumble all over themselves, but when they attend to what He reveals they are most blessed" (The Message).

I don't know about you, but I so desperately want to know and be a part of what God is doing in and through me. I hope you do too. I hope you get excited about your life and how much God wants to reveal his plan and Love for you!

"By faith Abraham left Egypt, not fearing the king's anger; he persevered because he saw Him Who is invisible" (Hebrews 11:27). I see Him . . . JESUS . . . Who is invisible . . . with my spiritual eyes. That is why I persevere! To persevere is to persist or continue in a course of action in spite of opposition, obstacles, or circumstances. I walk by faith and not by sight. Faith is the substance of things hoped for, the evidence of things unseen. By faith Abraham, when called to go to a place he would later receive as his inheritance, obeyed and went, even though he did not know where he was going (Hebrews 11:8). This is what I am doing right now: going by faith without knowing where. I love where God says in Hebrews 11:13–16 that all these people were still living by faith when they died. They admitted that they were aliens and strangers on earth; instead, they were longing for a better country—a heavenly one. Therefore God is not ashamed to be called their God, for He has prepared a city for them. Wow! How great and encouraging to know this world with all the sorrow and pain is not my real home. I also long for a heavenly one. I would rather choose to be mistreated along with the people of God than to enjoy the pleasures of sin for a short time. Oh, how short this earthly life really is! If we have hope only in this life, we are most miserable (1 Corinthians 15:19). "I have been crucified with Christ and I no longer live, but Christ lives in me. The life I live in my body, I live by Faith in the Son of God, who loved me and gave Himself for me" (Galatians 2:20, New International Version).

50

Pain and Growth
(May 26, 2018)

On May 14, 2018, we had our final three-hour court date and testimony to resolve financial matters after divorce. I still feel so much pain, as he not only betrayed me by divorce but wants to hurt me financially as well. I feel so demeaned and devalued over and over again by him. It takes so much energy out of me going through this unbelievable experience. I still cannot and probably never will understand this level of cruelty. I cry some more and then pray. I make a decision to forgive again and yet again when anger and revenge want to insert themselves into my thoughts and actions. Now it is up to the judge to make a decision on the facts and how she views the law. It is so painstaking to watch Tim as he tries to pretend that our marriage never happened. I try to move on as best I can, but I am beyond ready to this to be final and over!

I throw myself on the rock with my brokenness. That is the only way grace can pick up the broken pieces and use them as a whole. When I am weak and broken, I can speak into humanity, where we all live and cope with broken vessels of every kind. Jesus is the potter and I am the clay being molded every day into an image bearing more of His likeness. However, it is always a struggle between good and evil until we get rescued from this world someday. I am believing that people I touch will feel Jesus in me. I am so flawed, yet I am hanging onto his unfailing Love! When I am shaking and tossing as a leaf in the wind, I whisper, "please, sweet Jesus, just hold me." I feel desperate for my Prince of Peace. Sometimes I cannot be found until I get really lost and hurt beyond what I think is survivable. The minute I realize how terribly lost I am, the miracle of being found occurs. I begin to live in the supernatural realm with God. In and of myself it is not possible to attempt to heal and forgive the atrocities that happen to us all at some point in our lives.

God presents us with many growth opportunities. It seems to me that most of them come through difficulties and hardships. I wish that it was not so, but I do end up liking who I become when I am forced to press into God for my survival. That is why the great verse in James 1:2–4 can give us encouragement and insight into God's plan: "Consider it all joy, my brothers and sisters, whenever you face trials of many kinds, because you know that the testing of your faith produces perseverance. Let perseverance finish its work so that you may be mature and complete, not lacking anything." I like the end result of not lacking anything!

However, considering it all joy is the hard part. But God wants us mature with a testimony of knowing Him and experiencing His power of being with us and bringing us through whatever we face! There is no testimony without the tests. So when God allows anything difficult in our lives, we can be sure that the real danger or trouble lies in our response to it, and what we will lose if we run or rebel against it. Only with the tests can come splendid courage born of surrender and trust. What a tragedy and wasted potential for those who choose to run from God and what He wants them to become!

My ex-husband had a glorious opportunity to develop character and perseverance and to really experience God's power and miracles in his life. My heart is sad with his choice to run away from what God had planned. The good news, though, is that God is not finished with him yet, or me, or any of us as long as we have one breath left on this earth. I do and will continue to pray for him and his family. I pray for Godly sorrow that leads to repentance, forgiveness, and mercy at the foot of the cross. This is our only real hope. If we have hope only in this life, there is only misery. Preparing for eternity with eternal eyes is the most valuable insight we can have. God's Word trumps anything that we in our humanness without Him can come up with. When the enemy comes in like a flood, God promises to lift up a standard against him. I will not allow defeat or ever give in to the enemy.

In this world we will continue to have spiritual battles between choosing God or the devil. However, if we align ourselves with the One Who died, descended into hell, and took the keys of life and death from the enemy, we know that we are on the winning side. Don't ever lose sight of the fact that the devil is already a defeated foe. He just lies to us and doesn't want us to believe the truth. Yes, he is loose for a short time in this world to cause heartache, chaos, and many other things. His reign is short compared to our eternal eyes. Keep our eyes fixed on Jesus Who is the author and finisher of our faith!

I will soar again! It is a process of seeking Him, even when I am in incredible pain and labor pangs of growth. God will send me an eagle to remind me that I can rebound again and yet again. As often as I need to for life to be full of abundance and joy. God is allowing things in my life on purpose. All things work together for good because I love God and want to serve him (Romans 8:28).

I am feeding on a spiritual buffet. It is causing me to rise high above my circumstances. The supernatural and my invisible faith is becoming more real than the natural and visible world! I am beginning to see things from God's word and His purposes. God is giving me His Love to do the impossible: loving people while hating sin and evil that I see in them. I am thrilled to see that when I totally surrender to His power, the Holy Spirit does in me what I know I in the flesh could never do. I am losing the desire to react in the natural and less desire to take offense. There is an awareness of being fiercely loved by God. Aware of His high purpose for my life and what He wants me to become. The thrill of growing and becoming more like Jesus! A mighty warrior empowered for the front lines of battle is rising up in me. All my enemies are defeated, crushed, and under my feet. I believe that Jesus is seeking to perfect my faith. I have seen, and am in an impossible situation to force my faith to the surface.

Sooner or later the real Jesus will require me to look the impossible straight in the eye and believe God for His Power to show up in my life right where I am. In this very minute I will commit and obey. I will not back down. I have come too far to turn back now. My God has not changed even though my circumstances have. He is faithful to His Word and promises. I will look up to where the eagles fly high in the sky, safe from danger of their enemies. In Isaiah 40:31 it says this "But those who wait upon God get fresh strength. They spread their wings and soar like eagles, they run and don't get tired, they walk and don't lag behind" (The Message).

God is calling me to do something that I have never done before. Be still, my soul, and experience that He is God.

My Lord, My soul's Husband and Abba, Father. Lord, thank You for leading me toward a supernatural life versus a safe one. It is a calling out of expecting a familiar and predictable world. The increasing of faith for the power to reach the lost for You. I am standing on the edge of walking into my divine potential that You have ordained for me.

When we are in the very eye of the storm and unbearable pain, He preserves us. It is for sure not in this condition that He fails to come through the storm and grab our hand and pull us to safety. The safety is keeping us out of the claws of the enemy and not believing his lies. Safety is not letting anything come between us and God. It does not mean that we will not face giants in our lives. They come in many forms—cancer, fear, divorce, rejection, death and loss of those we love. The Bible says that in this world we will have trials and tribulations, but to be of good cheer because Jesus has overcome the world! That is great news indeed!

51

The Way of Love

Love is a choice, not a feeling. It's not that I believe we will never experience the magical feelings that falling in love brings. There is certainly nothing wrong with that and quite normal. But we must go at some point beyond that to discover the true depth of what real love is. What I want to express is something so very much deeper. It is when the doctor comes to inform you your husband of only one year has cancer at age twenty-five. Or when your child has been hit and killed by a drunk driver. Or perhaps your husband of only three years is divorcing you. There are so many bombs coming from all directions that test love long after the feelings are gone! Your sister, or brother, members of your own family betray you and threaten to crush the last breath of air that you breathe out of you. How and why will your love hold up under adverse conditions? When the anger and injustice builds to an intense rage and level you never could have imagined? I have had to come face to face personally and navigate this rugged terrain.

There are two basic choices. Learn the lessons of divine love, or let hate, bitterness and resentment take its course. Trust me, this is the hardest thing that I have ever done and will continue to do for the rest of my life:

to make a choice. One leads to life the other one to death. I know for sure that life is hard! I also know for sure that God is good, and the only real true source of Love that transcends all the crazy things that happen to us. We cannot control most events that come. What we can always control is how we choose to respond to them. I certainly will never say or imply that this is an easy feat. I will in fact state the opposite! It will most likely be the most difficult thing ever to achieve in this life! I do firmly believe, however, that it is and will be one of the most rewarding and exhilarating feelings once you get to the other side, see a light at the end of the tunnel, and be sure that the light is not that of a train coming. It is the supernatural light of experiencing God's Love that nothing else can ever come close to. This is to me one of the greatest verses and promises in the bible: John 3:16: For God so loved us that He sent His Son Jesus to die in our place so that we can live. To know God and His way of love is the most powerful force known to mankind.

Our love has limits. **God's love does not.**

Human love is an incredible thing, the gift that puts purpose in your life and happiness in your heart. God's love is even better! It is the one thing all of us seek in life, whether we realize it or not. If you have found yourself disillusioned with some goal you have chased for years, you may be beginning to understand the reason why. I know this is absolutely true for me at least. I was attempting to live life with my own wisdom and understanding apart from God. But the longing that you cannot put into words is always there. It is your soul's desire for God's divine, unconditional, eternal love! You can deny it, fight it, or try to ignore it, but God's love is the missing piece in the puzzle that is the authentic you. You will always be incomplete without it. John 15:13 says, "Love one another the way I have loved you. Greater love has no one than this that he lay down his life for his friends." Jesus laid down His life just for you. You are the apple of His eye!!

52

God Shows Up!

I love it when God shows up suddenly and unannounced in my everyday life. I was in the grocery store just mindlessly going about my shopping. I was rolling my cart down the aisle when I came across a woman on an electric cart right in the middle of my path. I was blocked. There was no way around her. She was staring at a large stack of Hamburger Helper boxes. She did not see. Her eyes were still glued to the many flavors before her. "Are you having trouble deciding which kind you want?" I asked her. "Oh no she responded." "I am on a fixed income and I was considering the price." I told her I understood as she moved out of the way for me to pass through. Just then I heard that still small voice of Jesus in my heart.

Pay for her groceries.

Wow! It took me by surprise, but it was so clear to me. I knew my Father's voice. I will be honest. At first I felt like protesting. The voices went something along the line of "This store is big. How could I find her again after moving on in the opposite direction?" So I finished up my shopping and headed for a register looking down every aisle for her. I didn't see her, so I wheeled into line at the register, telling myself I had done my part to find her. To my shock, there she was, right in front of me, loading her food on the belt! There is only excitement now from me now, knowing that only God could have timed and arranged this. Now she was speechless as I told the cashier that I was paying for her food. When she asked me why, I told her that God loves her, is crazy about her, and wants to show her that. I asked her whether she was aware of this wonderful Love from God. All she said was these three powerful words:

I am now!!

I will never forget it. What a joy I felt as she gave me a hug and a toothless smile!

53

A Memory
(July 26, 2017)

Today is my first day alone at Angie and Mark's house. I am watching the cat and watering plants while they are away. I will be here for a week. I feel lonely and want to reach out to Tim, my husband. But I realize that if I do that, I want something from him. I want him to fix my lonely feelings by reassuring me of how much he loves me and misses me. I want commitment and security from him. I know in reality he is unable and unwilling to meet my needs in our marriage. At this point all he talks about is wanting a divorce. So I am resisting my desire to contact him because I will get hurt by him again. Then I will feel even lonelier and worse than I do now by myself. I am working on being okay alone. I am practicing the peace and presence of God! I also called one of my friends for support. It is better to be alone and feel like a success than to be in a toxic relationship and feel like a failure. Tim is failing me now, but God never will. I encourage myself with His words from 1 Corinthians 2:9: "Eye hath not seen, nor ear heard, neither have entered into the heart of man, the things which God hath prepared for them that love him!"

54

A Risk of Faith

This is an amazing true story that I feel compelled to share with you. It will instill in you astounding hope for you and your situation, whatever it is!

Mark 5:21–34 (The Message)

After Jesus crossed over by boat, a large crowd met him at the seaside. One of the meeting-place leaders, named Jairus, came. When he saw Jesus, he fell to his knees, beside himself as he begged, "My dear daughter is at death's door. Come and lay hands on her so she will get well and live." Jesus went with him, the whole crowd tagging along, pushing and jostling Him.

A woman who had suffered a condition of hemorrhaging for twelve years—a long succession of physicians had treated her, and treated her badly, taking all her money and leaving her worse off than before—had heard about Jesus. She slipped in from behind and touched His robe. She was thinking to herself, "If I can put a finger on his robe, I can get well." The moment she did it, the flow of blood dried up. She could feel the change and knew her plague was over and done with.

At the same moment, Jesus felt energy discharging from him. He turned around to the crowd and asked, "Who touched my robe?"

His disciples said, "What are you talking about? With this crowd pushing and jostling you, you're asking, 'Who touched me?' Dozens have touched you!"

But he went on asking, looking around to see who had done it. The woman, knowing what had happened, knowing she was the one, stepped up in fear and trembling, knelt before him, and gave him the whole story.

Jesus said to her, "Daughter, you took a risk of faith, and now you're healed and whole. Live well, live blessed! Be healed of your plague."

Wow! I am awestruck and stunned by Jesus and the woman in this story. First of all, it reveals so much about Jesus' character and who He is. This is so critical for us to know. Even though He was rushing through the crowd to help a man whose daughter was dying, He stopped for her. Jesus is never too busy to stop for us. The disciples tried to dismiss it and move him along. But Jesus persisted and pursued this woman until she admitted it was she. I love these truths! Jesus is the same today with us. He is relentless with His persistent and steadfast love for us. He is thrilled when we respond to him and reach out with that risk of faith as this woman did. Another thing is how personal Jesus was and is. Each one of us is worth the whole world to Him. He sees the crowds but relates on a personal level to the individual. She got his full, undivided attention. That is so amazing that I cannot fully comprehend the character and love of our Lord. I believe the reason this story is told is to encourage us daily that we can trust Him with our life. No matter what is going on to break your heart, He is right there stopping for you! He will give you that one-on-one connection!

55

Finally Done
(December 1, 2018)

The judge has made a decision in the tragic divorce that I was forced to go through. It has been over a year of some really painful stuff. I am just glad it is over. I don't feel it was a fair settlement, but thankfully there is a higher Judge to whom he will answer someday. I accept it and be done.

God is taking care of me and I am blessed. I just recently got a part-time job driving a shuttle for a car dealership. I meet very nice customers and have an opportunity to share with them about Jesus' love. They drop off their cars to be serviced, and I take them to work or home. Then, when their car is done, I go get them and bring them back. It is a lot of driving but fun work.

A lot of healing has taken place, and I have moved on with my life. I am excited to see what God will do. I am wholly and fully committed to the will and purpose of God. Nothing less will do! There is no turning back once I have come so far and gone through so much. I hope this is true for you, my reader, also. I know we all have trials and pain. Our stories are the same and yet different. I want to encourage you to find hope and healing in the divine work of the cross! Jesus is still the answer and He always will be. He has the final say. God's Love runs deeper than the deepest ocean, He is not altered by the moods that we bring. For every problem He has a solution; He is consistently working behind the scenes. So whenever you feel like you're losing the battle and you want to just bow your head in defeat, remember, with God you are always the winner, for with Him by your side, you will never be beaten! Once you realize all that it cost God to forgive you, you will be held as in a vise, constrained by the Love of God! Every person on the face of this earth faces gaping Jaws of uncertainty. The only antidote to this poisonous threat is drawing closer to Jesus. The uncertainties of this world will eventually dissipate with the reassurance of our heavenly Father's presence. Resting in His Love and presence calms our anxious thoughts, anywhere at any time. Sometimes the greatest pain in our lives could be our greatest deliverance.

56

Four Men in the Furnace.

I am fiercely driven to share another true story with you! It kept me hanging onto the bottom of the rope when nothing solid was under my feet.

King Nebuchadnezzar built a gold statue, ninety feet high and nine feet thick. . . . He then ordered all the important leaders in the province, everybody who was anybody, to the dedication ceremony of the statue. They all came for the dedication, all the important people, and took their places before the statue that Nebuchadnezzar had erected.

A herald then proclaimed in a loud voice: "Attention, everyone! Every race, color, and creed, listen! When you hear the band strike up—all the trumpets and trombones, the tubas and baritones, the drums and cymbals—fall to your knees and worship the gold statue that King Nebuchadnezzar has set up. Anyone who does not kneel and worship shall be thrown immediately into a roaring furnace."

. . . Just then some Babylonian fortunetellers stepped up and accused the Jews. They said to King Nebuchadnezzar, "Long live the king!

You gave strict orders, O King, that when the big band started playing, everyone had to fall to their knees and worship the gold statue, and whoever did not go to their knees and worship it had to be pitched into a roaring furnace. Well, there are some Jews here—Shadrach, Meshach, and Abednego—whom you have placed in high positions in the province of Babylon. These men are ignoring you, O King. They don't respect your gods and they won't worship the gold statue you set up."

Furious, the King ordered Shadrach, Meshach, and Abednego to be brought in. When the men were brought in, the king asked them, "Is it true, Shadrach, Meshach, and Abednego, that you don't respect my gods and refuse to worship the gold statue that I have set up? I'm giving you a second chance—but from now on, when the big band strikes up, you must go to your knees and worship the statue that I have made. If you don't worship it, you will be pitched into a roaring furnace, no questions asked. Who is the god who can rescue you from my power?"

Shadrach, Meshach, and Abednego answered King Nebuchadnezzar, *"Your threat means nothing to us. If you throw us in the fire, the God we serve can rescue us from your roaring furnace and anything else you might cook up, O King. But even if he doesn't, it wouldn't make a bit of difference, O King. We still wouldn't serve your gods or worship the gold statue you set up."*

The King, his face purple with anger, ordered the furnace fired up seven times hotter than usual. He ordered some strong men from the army to tie them up, hands and feet, and throw them into the roaring furnace. Shadrach, Meshach, and Abednego, bound hand and foot, fully dressed from head to toe, were pitched into the roaring fire. Because the king was in such a hurry and the furnace was so hot, flames from the furnace killed the men who [threw them in], while the fire raged around Shadrach, Meshach, and Abednego.

Suddenly King Nebuchadnezzar jumped up in alarm and said, "Didn't we throw three men, bound hand and foot, into the fire?"

"That's right, O King," they said.

"But look!" he said. "I see four men, walking around freely in the fire, completely unharmed! And the fourth man looks like a son of the gods!"

The king went to the door of the roaring furnace and called in, "Shadrach, Meshach, and Abednego, servants of the High God, come out here!" The three men walked out of the fire.

All the important people, the government leaders and king's counselors, gathered around to examine them and discovered that the fire hadn't so much as touched the three men—not a hair singed, not a scorch mark on their clothes, not even the smell of fire on them!

Nebuchadnezzar said, "Blessed be the God of Shadrach, Meshach, and Abednego! He sent his angel and rescued his servants who trusted in him! They ignored the king's orders and laid their bodies on the line rather than serve or worship any god but their own. Therefore I issue this decree: Anyone anywhere, of any race, color, or creed, who says anything against the God of Shadrach, Meshach, and Abednego will be ripped to pieces, limb from limb, and their houses torn down. There has never been a god who can pull off a rescue like this."

Then the king promoted Shadrach, Meshach, and Abednego in the province of Babylon! (Daniel 3, The Message)

Wow! What a powerful story. God showed his power! The king converted to the real God and I can imagine the whole city also. I believe this miracle traveled far and near.

Now I know that we do not always get this kind of a miracle from God. The bottom line and point I want to make is this: I believed that God was able to deliver me from divorce and heal my marriage.

But even if he doesn't it wouldn't make a bit of a difference. I will still not bow down to, or worship false gods. I will worship the true God, miracle or not!

I will not receive the lie that is hissed into my ear that I am unlovable. I will also reject the temptation to believe that God doesn't Love me. These truths are so profound and powerful. But you and I both know how hard they are to digest and hold onto when the fire is turned up seven times hotter! I don't know all the pain and situations life has thrown your way. I do know I can understand to a great degree what you are going through. Life is very, very hard at times. However, I want to encourage you to fight along with me.

It is misleading to imagine that we are developed in spite of our circumstances; we are developed because of them. Maybe I got a miracle from God after all. But one of a different kind. I was not spared from experiencing another horrible, painful divorce. The miracle that I did get was experiencing God holding me and giving me supernatural strength to survive and thrive again in spite of it. The moment we recognize our complete weakness and our dependence upon Him will be the very moment that the Spirit of God will exhibit His power!

Perhaps the greatest miracle of all is when God exhibits His power in our life in whatever form or means. The impossibility for me became a reality. I have experienced a miracle! I am free! I am quieting myself, waiting and listening. I am being transformed into the image of God. "Be still and know that I am God" (Psalm 46:10).

God Gets the Last Word
1 Peter 5:8–11 (The Message)

Keep a cool head. Stay alert. The devil is poised to pounce, and would like nothing better than to catch you napping. Keep your guard up. You're not the only ones plunged into these hard times. It is the same for Christians all over the world. So keep a firm grip on the faith. The suffering won't last forever! It wouldn't be long before this generous God who has great plans for us in Christ—eternal and glorious plans they are!—will have you put together and on your feet for good. He gets the last Word, yes, he does!

God's Love is sticky, clinging to us. He will never let us go.

Once you have had a vision from God, you cannot go back. You may try as you will to be satisfied on a lower level, but God will never allow it. He will pursue you. He wants us to continue to press forward and into Him. With his Love and the indwelling of the Holy Spirit, nothing can stop the vision placed in our hearts and souls. I am pressing in to know God and His character. I want to watch what He does and learn from Him.

I have discovered that mostly what God does is simply Love us!! Hard to absorb but so true.

When I keep company with Him, I learn a lifestyle of Love. His Love was not cautious but extravagant. He didn't Love in order to get something from us but to give everything of Himself to us! I want to Love like this. I have a long way to go, but I am on the path. The path that leads to Joy and intimacy.

God spoke to me that healing comes from the inside out by the power of the Holy Spirit within me. I often look to people or outside myself for healing. That is also okay for healing, but the base, home plate, is where it all starts. The runs scored in baseball all start at home base and end there also. As I struggle with grief, pain, and loss, this is of great comfort to me. People and events on the outside will disappoint and let us down. Only the constant connection with Jesus and the Holy Spirit will last! It is the concrete base upon which everything else is built on. I am reminded of the story in the Bible of the two houses built. One was built on the sand and the other on the rock. When the storms and howling winds came, the one on the sand was destroyed but the one on the rock stood strong! (See Mathew 7:24–27 for the story.)

Life truly is a journey. Pain and Joy travel braided together. They cannot be separated. I believe a lot of God's jewels are crystallized tears. I know that there are thousands of mine in heaven! I am praying for and experiencing a divine collision with God: the explosion propelling me over and up, a supernatural ability to transcend my circumstances, which sometimes look bleak indeed. There is no guarantee either that life hands us an even balance of pain and Joy. At times the pain is so intense that just going into a coma and sleeping looks inviting. Then the Joy comes along when we are not expecting or looking for it. Often we face many challenges at the same time, A cocktail mix, if you will, of pain, hope, love, tears, grief, loss, joy. A strange feeling with these dual dynamics at work in us. Companionship and then solitude. Loneliness seems to be always lurking in the background for me. I believe that I am not alone in this. I see many of you walking alongside of me in this battle. Also, depression is not far behind. I try to surrender to God's divine will every day. It is the safest and softest pillow on which to rest our weary heads. The good news is that our stories can encourage us to press on and never give up! We all have the same story yet different. I can identify with Psalm 55 where David cries out to God in pain,

My insides are turned inside out; specters of death have me down.

I shake with fear, I shudder from head to foot.

"Who will give me wings," I ask—"wings like a dove?"

Get me out of here on dove wings;

I want some peace and quiet.

I want a walk in the country,

I want a cabin in the woods.

I'm desperate for a change from rage and stormy weather.

(The Message)

I would encourage you to read the whole chapter. It is filled with more raw feelings as he had been betrayed by his best friend. All his life he trusted him and he became a traitor. The pain continues as he pleads to God for help. I also hear fierce anger in this: "Haul my betrayers off alive to hell and let them experience the horror, let them feel every desolate detail of a damned life." "Come down hard, Lord—slit their tongues" (The Message). Wow, I have felt this as well with the betrayal of my ex-husband. Finally, when tired and spent, David utters to God: "I trust in you!"

57

The Rock

Here is a poem I wrote in August 2018:

I am okay even when I feel like I am not.
I am holding onto the solid rock.
Jesus is my solid rock,
I am okay even when I feel like I am not.
I am holding onto the knot
at the end of the rope,
Jesus is my only hope.
I will not let go, I will never stop.
Jesus is my solid rock.
Jesus is holding me up on the top,
I can trust this solid rock.
I know life is no easy street.
I can go on because He is under my feet.
Without this rock I cannot stand,
I would be on sinking sand.

When my path is hard and I cannot see,
Jesus my rock is there for me.
Sometimes I feel that I cannot go on anymore,
then I hear Jesus knocking on my door.
"I am still your rock, I have guided you before.
You can take one step more,
each one gets you closer to that heavenly shore."

It is good to bring our problems and concerns to God. He always listens, cares, and answers us. Also sometimes we need to talk to our problems about God. Remind them that God is bigger and stronger than they. Tell them what God has already said about them. For example, you can talk to fear, and tell it that it is no longer welcome in your life. God has already said in His Word that he has not given us the Spirit of fear but of Love, Power, and a sound mind!

So if it didn't come from God, you don't want it!

That means it is coming from a dark place like the enemy. Fear is one of the strongest tools used against us. At least it has been a major struggle for me. God's Word is powerful and sharper than any two-edged sword. We can speak God's Word directly to our struggles. That does not mean our emotions and pain get an instant fix, but over and over again the reminder of Who is in control helps. I love using the verse in the Bible that say, "Greater is He that is in us then he that is in the world." What a comforting promise! Jesus descended into the pit of hell Himself and took the keys away from the devil after the crucifixion. Then he arose victorious, setting us free from sin. The last enemy to be conquered is death. Then all who receive it will never die again! As the letter to the Hebrews says, "it is appointed unto man once to die and then the judgment." If we have Jesus, if we have accepted Jesus into our hearts, we need not fear the judgment. We will hear the words of life. Jesus will say to us: "Enter in and enjoy what I have prepared for you from the beginning of time."

Eternal life! Make sure that you are ready to meet God!

So we are not giving up. How could we! Even though on the outside it often looks like things are falling apart on us, on the inside, where God is making new life, not a day goes by without His unfolding grace. These hard times are small potatoes compared to the coming good times, the lavish celebration prepared for us. There's far more here than meets the eye. The things we see now are here today, gone tomorrow. But the things we can't see now will last forever! (2 Corinthians 4:16–18, The Message)

Count on it: Everyone who had it in for you will end up out in the cold—real losers. Those who worked against you will end up empty-handed—nothing to show for their lives. When you go out looking for your old adversaries you won't find them—not a trace of your old enemies, not even a memory. That's right. Because I, your God, have a firm grip on you and I'm not letting go. I'm telling you, "Don't panic. I'm right here to help you" (Isaiah 41:11–13, The Message)

So let God work His will in you. Yell a loud no to the Devil and watch him scamper. Say a quiet yes to God and He will be there in no time. Quit dabbling in sin. Purify your inner life. Quit playing the field. Hit bottom, and cry your eyes out. The fun and games are over. Get serious, really serious. Get down on your knees before the Master; it is the only way you will get on your feet (James 4:7–10, The Message)

Wow, I have really experienced these truths. I sure have cried my eyes out before God with pain, grief, loss. Part of healing and saving my life, getting on my feet again was this. Getting serious with my life before the Master.

I have nothing apart from Him. In realizing this I now know that I have everything.

So comforting also to know that God is taking care of my enemies. I believe a part of me will always hurt, but this is as good as it gets in our fallen, sin-filled world. God gave mankind free will, but sometimes free will hurts. When my husband rejected me and chose divorce, it crushed me. However, Love is not real if it is forced and not by a free decision of the will. I have a love/hate relationship with free will.

Gracious Uncertainty
By Oswald Chambers

My natural inclination is to be so precise—trying always to forecast accurately what will happen next—that I look upon uncertainty as a bad thing. I think that I must reach some predetermined goal, but that is not the nature of the spiritual life. The nature of the spiritual life is that we are certain in our uncertainty. Consequently, we do not put down roots. Our common sense says, "Well, what if I were in that circumstance?" We cannot presume to see ourselves in any circumstance in which we have never been.

Certainty is the mark of the commonsense life—*gracious uncertainty* is the mark of the spiritual life. To be certain of God means that we are uncertain in all our ways, not knowing what tomorrow may bring. This is generally expressed with a sigh of sadness, but it should be an expression of breathless expectation. We are uncertain of the next step, but we are certain of God. As soon as we abandon ourselves to God and do the task He has placed closest to us, He begins to fill our lives with surprises. When we become simply a promoter or a defender of a particular belief, something within us dies. That is not believing God—it is only believing our belief about him. Jesus said, "Unless you become as little children" (Matthew 18:3). The spiritual life is the life of a child. We are not uncertain of God, just uncertain of what He is going to do next. If my certainty is only in our beliefs, we develop a sense of self-righteousness, become overly critical, and are limited by the view that our beliefs are complete and settled. But when we have the right relationship with God, life is full of spontaneous, joyful uncertainty and expectancy. . . . Leave everything to Him and it will be gloriously and graciously uncertain how He will come in—but you can be certain that He will come. Remain faithful to Him!

I like the way Brené Brown put it in her book *Rising Strong:*

I agree that it is better to have loved and lost than never to have loved at all. But heartbreak knocks the wind out of you, and the feelings of loss and longing can make getting out of bed a monumental task. Learning to trust and lean in to love again can feel impossible. Yes, if we care enough and dare enough, we will experience disappointment. But in those moments when disappointment is washing over us and we're desperately trying to get our heads and hearts around what is or is not going to be, the death of our expectations can be painful beyond measure! As difficult as it is we must embrace the emotion of falling, pain and loss. There are too many people today who instead of feeling hurt are acting out their hurt; instead of acknowledging pain, they are inflicting pain on others. Rather than risking feeling disappointed, they're choosing to live disappointed.

I am learning that I cannot run from or avoid suffering. My focus now is to suffer without giving up. It is also tempting to become hard, resentful, bitter, and revengeful. I want to stay soft, compassionate, forgiving, gentle, and loving! Perhaps this may be the greatest miracle of all after everything that you and I have been through. I know that I am not finished yet, but I have faith in God to keep me one day at a time. Someday we will get rescued from this fallen world!

I would like to share with you some more insights about wholehearted living from Brené Brown in Rising Strong:

Choosing to live and love with our whole hearts is an act of defiance. You are going to confuse, tick off, and terrify lots of people including yourself.

I define *wholehearted living* as engaging in our lives from a place of worthiness. It means cultivating the courage, compassion, and connection to wake up in the morning and think, *No matter what gets done and how much is left undone, I am enough.*

My thought here is this is true because of the definition of who Jesus says we are. He is the only one Who defines us truthfully. Yes, I am imperfect and vulnerable and sometimes afraid, but that doesn't change the truth that I am also brave and worthy of Love and belonging. I believe the heart of the matter is that we as humans crave three basic things. They are Love, belonging and worthiness.

The willingness to tell our stories, feel the pain of others, and stay genuinely connected in this disconnected world is not something that we can do halfheartedly. To practice courage, compassion, and connection is to look at life and the people around us, and say, I am all in!

Owning our story and *loving ourselves through that process* is the bravest thing we will ever do!

It sure is the bravest thing that I have ever done!

When we let go of what other people think and own our story, we gain access to our worthiness, which is the feeling that we are enough just as we are and that we are worthy of love and belonging. It is a must to love ourselves. Shame, blame, disrespect, betrayal, and the withholding of affection damage the roots from which love grows. Love can survive these injuries only if they are acknowledged, healed, and the behavior changed.

I want to interject my own experience here that my now ex-husband was not willing to do this. Our relationship was doomed because of his abuse, withholding of affection, and all those things I mentioned. I do know that when you betray someone or behave in an unkind way toward them, you are not practicing love! It really hurts!! For me I don't want someone who says they love me, I want someone who practices that love for me every day! I choose to see rejection as re-direction. I decide to Love as if I have never been hurt!

When we deny our stories and disengage from tough emotions, they don't go away; instead they own us, and they define us. Our job is not to deny the story, but to defy the ending—to rise strong, recognize our story, and rumble with the truth until we get to a place where we think, yes. This is what happened. This is my truth. And I will choose how this story ends.

There is no shame attached. All of my experiences have come together to make up who I am. I live by the belief that nothing is wasted. The harshness of winter is necessary to bring about the beauty of spring.

Authenticity is the daily practice of, to cite another of Brown's books, letting go of who we think we're supposed to be and embracing who we really are. Staying real is one of the most courageous battles that we will ever fight. I certainly can attest to this when my self-esteem, worthiness, and belonging were violently trampled on. I am in the process of this fight that lasts a lifetime of acknowledging who I am and living in that freedom. When I am alone through suffering, heartbreak, temptation, disappointment, sickness, thwarted desires, or a broken relationship, and I am totally speechless, unable to ask even one more question of God—that is when He just comes close and holds me. He starts to teach me that His presence is enough.

I will never understand, nor should I try to make sense of, all the suffering in this world. Especially the innocent little children with cancer among other things. It breaks my heart! But the best response, and the only response that I know of, is to believe and know that Jesus is enough! If we don't believe this, what else is there? Where else can we go but to the Lord?

58

Faith under Pressure

Consider it pure joy, my brothers and sisters, whenever you face trials of many kinds, because you know that the testing of your faith produces perseverance. Let perseverance finish its work so that you may be mature and complete, not lacking anything (James 1:2–4, King James Version).

I have a love—conflicting—uncomfortable—pushback feeling about this verse. I love it because I know it to be true as the word of God and personal experience. But it is conflicting, as I do not consider it pure joy when I am heartbroken and crying. I feel it as a gut-wrenching experience. Continuing losses and disappointment are occurring in my life right now. Others that I love are in pain. I push back, not wanting to embrace the journey of pain and disappointments of life. I am uncomfortable with the process of pain and joy traveling together. Yet they do and always will in this life.

The part I do focus on is the end result, which I really want and need. Perseverance, maturity, completeness, not lacking anything all sound very powerful to me. These are the tools that will keep me from sinking and giving into the uncertainty and challenges of life. I keep meditating on "not lacking anything" and think impossible. Yet the power this verse holds must be looked at. As I reflect and struggle, I believe you can identify with me in many ways. I am sure you, my readers, are going through hard, tough, impossible stuff also. I want this to encourage you that you are not alone. We are all in this together. God gives us His promise that when the enemy comes in like a flood, the Lord will raise up a standard against him. God's word is an indispensable weapon against evil. The best standard that God has provided is what He has already spoken. He will continue to speak today through the Holy Spirit.

> Jesus was despised and rejected, a man of sorrows, acquainted with deepest grief. We turned our backs on him and looked the other way. He was despised, and we did not care (Isaiah 53:3, New Living Translation).

> Keep your eyes on Jesus, Who both began and finished this race we're in. Study how He did it. Because He never lost sight of where He was headed—that exhilarating finish in and with God—He could put up with anything along the way: Cross, shame, whatever. And now He's there, in the place of honor, right alongside God. When you find yourselves flagging in your faith, go over that story again (Hebrews 12:2–3, The Message)

Study again what Jesus went through. The pleading in the garden of Gethsemane to take the cross and death away from Him. The last sentence he uttered before his arrest was "Nevertheless, not my will but Yours be done." The only way I found to bear my cross is to focus on the joy that is set before me at the end. *Eternal life and heaven! That is where it all ends and begins!*

I am post-divorce now for fifteen months. It still hurts but not in the forefront of my life. I am making new connections. New connections require emotional and physical safety. *We can't be vulnerable and open with* people *who are hurting us.* I am learning to select carefully whom I share with and let into my heart and inner world. I can tell fairly quickly with the way someone responds to me whether they are safe or not. Sometimes I get it wrong but make corrections as I go. None of us is perfect, and that is perfectly okay.

The ideal and my heart's desire is to prosper after failure and to get stronger, not weaker, when I encounter adversity. I am sure you as my readers have the same longing. But as I have experienced, this is easy to say and much harder to practice and do. As the cumulative hurts pile up year after year, it feels nearly impossible. I have had so many tears that at times seem unending.

I get hope and encouragement from what David says to the Father in Psalm 56:8 (New Living Translation): "You keep track of all my sorrows. You have collected all your tears in Your bottle. You have recorded each one in Your book!" Wow, what empathy from our Lord and Savior! I will never get anything even close to this in my life on this earth.

Another promise that I hold onto daily is Isaiah 43:2: "When you go through deep waters, I will be with you. When you go through rivers of difficulty, you will not drown. When you walk through the fire of oppression, you will not be burned up; the flames will not consume you" (New Living Translation). Similarly, 2 Corinthians 4:8–9, 16 (New International Version): "We are hard pressed on every side, but not crushed; perplexed, but not in despair; persecuted, but not abandoned; struck down, but not destroyed. . . . Therefore we do not lose heart. Though outwardly we are wasting away, yet inwardly we are being renewed day by day."

Life will always tend to be the nature of a roller coaster. Ups and downs traveling together to form this ride called our lives.

I will never totally get over my grief, pain, and loss, but a new normal will occur. I will learn to live with it. That is as good as it gets, in my opinion and experience. I have also learned that the hard work of healing is worth it. The struggles eventually pay off. Everything we get has a price tag attached to it. Character is formed. Contentment comes at times. Sometimes joy. Always hope based on the future not this life. The Bible says that if we have hope only in this life we are most miserable. I believe one hundred percent that it is the truth for sure.

So we are not giving up. How could we? Even though on the outside it often looks like things are falling apart on us, on the inside, where God is making new life, not a day goes by without his unfolding grace. These hard times are small potatoes compared to the coming good times, the lavish celebration prepared for us. There's far more here than meets the eye. The things we see now are here today, gone tomorrow. But the things we cannot see now will last forever (2 Corinthians 4:16–18, The Message).

I was in the grocery store parking lot walking toward the store one day when I caught up to a man whistling. I could not tell you what song it was. I can say what feelings came over me. There was a fleeting moment of happiness. It was beautiful. Like hearing a peaceful songbird. All seemed well with the world and my life. I spoke with him and said I liked it. He replied he does it all the time. It is now an unconscious act and a part of who he is and his identity. He was not even aware of his whistling and that it was overheard by me or the effect it had on me. I called him the "whistling ministry man." Just a simple thing that never crossed my mind before. An unexpected blessing. He may never know the uplifting that I felt. Two people going for groceries and intersecting ever so briefly, but in some strange way a very profound experience.

Right now my life is stable. I am doing well in my part-time job as a shuttle driver for a local Ford dealership. When people drop off their cars for service I take them to work, home, or wherever they want to go. When their car is finished, they call me, and I pick them up and transport them back to the dealer to pick up their vehicle. I like it most of the time. Sometimes it is a bit overwhelming if it gets too busy and people are all wanting to go in different directions. I have to work that out with them who goes first and last. For the majority of the time, people are nice and it works out. It does take some energy out of me, though, because I feel responsible for the safety of others. I tend to drive differently at work then when I am by myself. I believe that is a good thing. Maybe I will drive slower when I am on my own also because of my job.

59

The Truth about Self-Worth!

This is of utmost importance to me and, I believe, to almost all of us, especially women. In the beginning (Gen. 1:26–27), God created man and woman in His image. We are made in His likeness. He said that everything He made was very good! I want to expose the enemy and his lies to us about our self-esteem. We need to see ourselves as God sees us, not the messages of this world and their standards. The world says that your worth is based on many false ideas. Money, job, material things, sex, the big house with a white picket fence. There are many other things that the devil whispers to us that we must have to be worth anything.

So reject the image of the world and the lies that come with it. We must see ourselves as God's children. We are loved, forgiven, and precious just as we are. The temptation is to view ourselves through the lens of how others have treated us instead of how God treats us and sees us. The Bible says we will know the truth and it will set us free. There is no other freedom but the truth. God says that we are deserving of unconditional Love because of what Jesus has done on the cross. When He died the last words he cried out were "It is finished," and indeed it was and always will be. There is nothing more that we can add or take away to become worthy of Love.

The image of God is a foundational concept for understanding our significance and purpose. Understanding how we are made in God's image helps us to see the basis for the dignity and purpose of our life and work. Our worth is connected to our creator. If God is of great and inestimable worth, then human beings made in His image must be of great value too! To attack a person is to attack God through His image bearer. James 3:9 also reminds us that human beings are made in God's image: With the tongue we bless our Lord and Father, and with it we curse men and women who have been made in the likeness of God. This verse reminds us that how we treat people is an indication of how we value God. There are no ordinary people. Even the most obscure person in not ordinary in God's eyes. We share God's characteristics. You don't need to prove to anyone how valuable you are. The cross speaks louder than your words, your doubts, your accomplishments, and your possessions. The creator of the universe died for you on the cross. Jesus shed His blood. He knows you and He loves you. You are not your past mistakes, you are not your past sins. You have been redeemed by the blood. God's love is not based on your performance. God's mercy is not dependent on you. Christ has become our righteousness. His love is going to keep you to the end. He sees every tear, he knows your name. He knows the number of hairs on your head! He knew you and saw you before you were even born. Psalm 139:14 says that we are fearfully and wonderfully made.

Not one drop of my self-worth depends on someone else's acceptance of me. If you find yourself constantly trying to prove your worth to someone, you have already forgotten your value! "Your value does not decrease based on someone's inability to see your worth" (Zig Ziglar). Make sure you don't start seeing yourself through the eyes of those who don't value you. *Know your worth even if they don't! I don't have time to hate people who hate me because I am too busy loving the people who love me!* Life is short and precious. Take responsibility for creating your own happiness, well-being, and self-worth. Then you own it. Don't ever let anyone take it away from you!

Jesus is our example of how to treat people. He lived it on earth for 33 years. I want to highlight the times of Jesus interacting with women.

He stood up for them against harsh men and abuse. Jesus valued them and validated their worth way back in a time when for sure that was unheard of and radical. There are many, but I want to briefly highlight three of them that stand out to me.

The first one is the woman at the well found in John chapter 4. I will just put in my own words the main point. First off, she was a Samaritan woman, and Jews did not talk to them. Jesus asked her for a drink from her well. She was awestruck also that Jesus, a Jew, would ask her for water. Jesus went on to ask her to bring her husband here also to the well. She replied that she had no husband. Jesus said, "I agree. You have had five husbands, and the one you are living with now is not your husband." Jesus knew all about her and there was no condemnation or shame. Jesus just shared with her the good news that he was the Savior and she could have living water and never thirst again. Just then His disciples came back from buying lunch. They were shocked. They could not believe he was talking with that kind of a woman. No one said what they were all thinking, but their faces showed it. The woman was so excited that she left her water-pot and ran into the village to tell everyone what had happened. *"Come see a man who knew all about the things I did, who knows me inside and out. Do you think this could be the Messiah?"* Wow! How awesome that the love and acceptance of Jesus won this woman to become a believer and tell the whole city. I think the key here is to be fully known and fully loved. There is nothing greater than unconditional Love!!

The second woman is found in John 8:1–11 (The Message):

The religion scholars and Pharisees led in a woman who had been caught in an act of adultery. They stood her in plain sight of everyone and said, "Teacher, this woman was caught red-handed in the act of adultery. Moses, in the Law, gives orders to stone such persons. What do you say?" . . . Jesus bent down and wrote with His finger in the dirt. They kept at Him, badgering Him. He straightened up and said, "The sinless one among you, go first: Throw the stone." . . . Hearing that, they walked away, one after another . . . The woman was left alone. Jesus stood up and spoke to her. "Woman, where are they? Does no one condemn you?" She replied, "No one, Master." "Neither do I," said Jesus. "Go on your way. From now on, don't sin."

Wow! What an advocate for protecting women and the brilliant lesson that none of us are without sin and all need forgiveness. None of us can cast the first stone!

The final story is found in John 12:1–8 (The Message), where Jesus was invited to Martha, Mary, and their brother Lazarus' home for dinner.

Mary came in with a jar of very expensive aromatic oils, anointed and massaged Jesus' feet, and then wiped them with her hair. The fragrance of the oils filled the house.

Judas Iscariot, one of his disciples, was there also. He complained and said all that money she had spent on the oil could have been given to the poor instead.

Jesus said, "Let her alone! . . . You always have the poor with you. You don't always have me."

What an awesome scene that must have been. One greater example of how Jesus viewed, respected, protected, and loved women. This is still God's heart today for how to treat women and all other humans made in His image and likeness. If you have seen Jesus, you have seen God.

This is the crisis that we are in. God is light and streamed it into the world, but men loved darkness better than light because their deeds were evil. They hated the light, fearing a painful exposure. Abuse survives in secrecy and darkness, like all evil. It must be brought to the light so it can be seen and stopped. Everyone living in the truth wants the light to shine on their life because they have nothing to hide. If you or anyone you know is living in the pain and darkness of abuse, bring it to the light! There is never an excuse for abuse!!

I am experiencing a fierce hunger to know God and walk with Him. I want to see His power in and through me! I don't need to worry about tomorrow because God is already there. Nothing hurts my heart more than lost souls. I believe that is in the heart of Jesus also. What agony it must have been for Him to suffer and die for us only to have His beloved reject the free gift of salvation and eternal life. How extremely tragic!

> The irony is that we attempt to disown our difficult stories to appear more whole or more acceptable, but our wholeness—even our wholeheartedness—actually depends on the integration of all of our experiences, including the falls. (Brené Brown)

I commit to move forward beyond abuse. I commit to overcome divorce and the evil that brought it about. I commit to heal, forgive, and Love again!

As Brené says, we write our own daring endings. We craft Love from heartbreak, compassion from shame, grace from disappointment, and courage from failure. We are the brave and brokenhearted. We are rising strong!!

Epilogue
To You, My Readers

I have two deep desires for you. My first one is that by sharing my life's story with you it has given you the knowledge that you do not walk alone. Every one of us has a different journey, but the one constant thing will be challenges and tough times. I hope that I have connected with you in a way that has helped you in whatever you have or will face in the future. Sometimes you will be high on the mountain feeling, thrilled by the view. Then a deep valley experience of pain, mourning or loss will occur. This is the nature of this flawed world that we live in. My heart for you is not only to encourage you in this life but to make sure you are ready to live forever in the next.

This leads me into my deepest and most passionate prayer for all of you. First and foremost, above all I, want my life's story to change where you spend eternity. To know that you, my readers, will accept Jesus Christ as your Lord and Savior was and is my ultimate purpose and desire when writing my story. I want you to choose heaven as your final home. If you already have, I rejoice with you! This world is not your home; you are just here for a short time. God loves you more than you can ever imagine!

Make that decision today before you put this book away. It is the single most urgent choice that you will make in your life! I pray for you that God will speak to your heart, draw you close, comfort you, and hold you!

The heart of my story is about pain, healing, faith, forgiveness, and learning to love no matter how hard life is. I had to forgive myself for the many poor choices I made as well as my Dad for his abuse. My hope is that you will be inspired to work hard and trust God with your life. God will forgive you and give you strength to heal, forgive yourself, and others. He will walk with you every minute of every day just like he did with me!

God Bless You All,
Ruth Redcay

You can email me at: relladelia@outlook.com
I would love to hear from you!!

Ruth Redcay

About the Author

Ruth Redcay currently resides in Newark, Delaware. She is blessed to have a close relationship with family and friends. She is active in the local church. She also goes on yearly mission trips to Jamaica.

Ruth enjoys table tennis several times a week as well as bowling. Her passion is sharing the love of Jesus with those who do not know him!